The Access to Public Information

The Access to Public Information:

A Fundamental Right

By

Alejandra Soriano Diaz

Cambridge
Scholars
Publishing

The Access to Public Information: A Fundamental Right

By Alejandra Soriano Diaz

This book first published 2024

Cambridge Scholars Publishing

Lady Stephenson Library, Newcastle upon Tyne, NE6 2PA, UK

British Library Cataloguing in Publication Data
A catalogue record for this book is available from the British Library

ISBN: 978-1-0364-1521-1
ISBN (Ebook): 978-1-0364-1522-8

CONTENTS

PRESENTATION vii

INTRODUCTION 1
The importance of information for citizens 1
The State and the right of access to public information 13

INFORMATION IN THE CONTEXT OF FUNDAMENTAL RIGHTS 16
Historical recognition 16
Information Law and Human Rights 25

PUBLIC INFORMATION: BUILDING A CONCEPT 32
Authorized and responsible parties 36
Public interest test 42
Reasonableness test 46
Principles 50
Characteristics of public information 58

EXCEPTIONS REGIME 69
Personal Data Protection 70
Public Interest Exceptions 87

OBLIGATIONS OF THE STATE 100
Duty to Actively Produce Information 107
Obligation to Investigate Violations of Rights 113

ENVIRONMENTAL INFORMATION, COLLECTIVE RIGHTS AND ACCESS TO JUSTICE 117
Access to Environmental Information 120
Collective rights of indigenous peoples in America 125
Relationship between Information and Access to Justice 135

ENFORCEMENT 147
Information Ombudsman 148
Judicial Mechanisms 152
Access to Public Information Action 154
Habeas Data Action 156

AN UNFINISHED BUSINESS 160

BIBLIOGRAPHY 163

PRESENTATION

How important is information for the human being that even God left the gift of prophecy for us to understand His designs. *To know* is inherent to the human *being* and the search for knowledge is equivalent to the historical development of humanity. All civilizations show a deep respect for the wisdom that constitutes a treasure that is jealously guarded, imparted to members of the same clan, shared with allies, and hidden from enemies. Alienating a community from the information that is vital to it is the same as reducing it to a herd that grazes in the fields until it is led to the slaughterhouse. An uninformed society is easily manipulated, it becomes a mere consumer of other people's ideas and, therefore, it ends up being deprived of its freedom of thought, of the ability to create and to decide about its own life and future. Political participation and social development depend, to a large extent, on having timely and quality information about the facts that interest its members. And this interest cannot be understood superficially: not only what the individual or the group finds *interesting* or *entertaining* is of interest to them, but everything that can influence their lives and those of future generations. Therefore, the decision on *what* to inform about should be made on a wide range of data and under the principle of good faith. Any restrictions to the dissemination of information may only be made on an exceptional basis.

An informed society is also a favorable scenario for social peace because the production of ideas calls for dialogue to resolve the conflicts inherent to coexistence, while secrecy and obscurity produce distrust and rejection, fostering resistance that can lead to intolerance and even sectarianism. Societies that value democracy more highly have promoted more open political-administrative systems, aware of the need for the people to call their governments to account. Thus, transparency ratifies that those who govern are at the service of society and not the other way around. An example of this openness is Argentina, a country which, after a bloody phase of military dictatorship and secrecy, is today striving for an open society where *accountability* is at the core of all public functions. Another example that can be cited is the impulse of the Nordic countries, with a marked tendency towards openness, far from the hermetism that authorities usually tend to, which advocated a Europe more open to its inhabitants through the right of access to the documents of the European Parliament and the Council. As Rams Ramos (2008) recalls:

> The evolution of this right starts from its exclusive recognition for access to documents, understood in a very restrictive way, kept in historical archives, access that was also subject to very broad exclusions. It is, fundamentally, the strength of the Member States with a tradition of openness - such as Sweden, Denmark, the Netherlands and Finland - that will give a definitive impulse to the development and recognition of the right of access. [But] The open-minded countries could not impose their criteria on those more reticent about transparency, and the truth is (...) that it has taken a long time for the concept of access to information as a subjective right to become generalized in the domestic constitutional law of the States.

A society that is unwilling to confront its reality and to take action, cannot be considered truly free. Freedom, today, faces serious information challenges: we find ourselves in the overlapping dystopias of Aldous Huxley and George Orwell, in which we are constantly bombarded by so much news that it is difficult to discern the real and important from the fallacy and waste. Meanwhile, in this endless sea of data, entire governments –not only the official ones but also the de facto ones– sail armored, *appropriating* information and acting as a true *Thought Police,* controlling which and how much information is delivered to the people who are, for all intents and purposes, its true owners. To apprehend this reality is the first step to snatch the right to information and its main form of exercise: the access to it.

Access to information acts as a two-tiered right. On the one hand, access itself *is* a fundamental right because it constitutes a vindication of the power of the people, of their right to ownership of *public property* and of the right to *know* what the government does in their behalf. On the other hand, it is an intermediate or auxiliary tool to reach other fundamental rights, because it empowers the exercise of other prerogatives, from holding those in power accountable, to deciding how many children to have. Every decision is nourished by information and the quality of this information will increase the probability of success, that is, the probability of achieving the individual and common objectives proposed by a person, a family, a community or an entire nation. And although everything goes *through* information and is fed by it, it is the prerogative of its legitimate owner to use it or not in his or her favor, to use it *against* a certain person or situation, or to ignore it completely. But it is *their* choice. The right to information gives life to that *choice* and is therefore linked to personal freedom.

Although information -and its dissemination- is commonly associated with journalistic work, its impact on other areas of social life is decisive for social, scientific and technological progress and for improving standards in the exercise of human rights. Among others, information is particularly relevant for collective rights. One of the first groups to understand the intrinsic relationship between good quality and truthful information and the protection of other fundamental rights was that of consumers. Deceptive advertising has been controlled by states for decades, and the protection of consumers' rights to make an informed choice of the goods and services they purchase has become increasingly rigorous. Although it is not a finished issue and it is evident that there are still abuses of consumer rights, it cannot be denied that this relationship between the *choice* made and the information received by an individual is still incipient in other branches of law. Today, the parameters on production and dissemination of environmental information are a paradigm for ancestral communities and propose a point of balance and encounter (or break, depending on the approach adopted by peoples and governments) for public decision making on non-renewable natural resources and other productive activities.

The research contained in this book goes through the legislative advances of countries such as the United Kingdom, Argentina, Mexico and Ecuador, finding in each of them interesting characteristics for the protection of the right of access to public information, as well as important contrasts to form creative solutions to the conflicts it entails. The aim is not to exemplify but to provide a window into possibilities that might otherwise remain outside analysis. This is not to say that there are no highly valuable schemes for the development of this right in other legislations and societies: in Europe as well as in America, Asia and Africa, important progress has been made in achieving transparency, especially from the perspective of the fight against corruption. Sweden, the birthplace of Anders Chydenius, is the pioneer country in positivizing access to public information in the Freedom of the Press Act of 1766, and it has continued its tradition of openness to this day. Nor can the Freedom of Information Act of the United States, passed in 1966, be overlooked, with which the so-called "first wave" of legislations guaranteeing access to information began, mainly in the 1970s, and with which access as a *right* began to spread worldwide. In South Africa, the law on access to public information was a grain of sand to support the post-apartheid process, according to Pansy Tlakula, that country's Information Regulator, in 2022. And what not to say about Australia (one of the countries in Oceania with specific legislation on access to public information), which recognizes that information is "*a valuable national* resource"[1] , a category that is very important to understand that its gathering and processing is subject to the achievement of public functions, and its property remains in *the people*.

This work also reflects some of the relevant rulings of the supranational courts of both Europe and the Americas, which reflect the legal culture of these two continents. At the same time, reports of the United Nations special rapporteurs, as well as the general observations of the specialized committees, are relevant instruments for interpreting and applying the rules on access, on the one side, and on secrecy and confidentiality in the opposithe shore, in a way that is compatible with the human rights catalog. All these instruments enrich the formation of opinions on this important subject, not only from the legal aspect -providing argumentative tools- but also from the social approach, since they allow consideration of the origins, trajectory and destiny toward which states are heading.

This book is dedicated to my father –once silenced and persecuted by the dictatorship– who devoted his youth to social communication and spent his life teaching me that information is power.

[1] Office of the Australian Information Commissioner 2011.

INTRODUCTION

The importance of information for citizens

- A mother is searching for her son who has apparently been swallowed by the earth.
- A widow demands to know the circumstances under which her husband died, since he had uncovered a corruption scheme prior to his decease.
- Three families are demanding that the violent murders of their daughters be clarified and that the perpetrators be punished.
- A non-governmental organization is concerned about the distribution of drugs introduced into the country without knowing for certain their safety for human health.
- An indigenous community claims to maintain ancestral possession of a territory while the public deeds of the same area prove the ownership of third parties.
- A company needs the public file that resulted in a large fine against it in order to challenge it and defend itself.

Each of these cases is real. In each of them, reliable and timely information was essential to achieve justice, to exercise other human rights, or to avoid an escalation of violence. In each of them, indispensable information was either unavailable or denied by the state.

Information has an immeasurable value for today's society. Although knowledge has had a great value for personal and collective development throughout the history of human beings, the truth is that in the digital era, the flow of information and the utility that everyone gives to it is becoming more and more concrete. Obtaining accurate and timely data can make a marked difference in the life of a person, a family, a neighborhood and even a generation. While this statement can be easily understood in the field of commerce, where multimillion-dollar transactions are made daily with data banks of various kinds, its recognition in the framework of fundamental rights has been a lengthy process, despite the increase in its social relevance. Strangely, it has even slowed down, with academic production and casuistry on this subject proving to be lower in 2024 than in the previous two decades.

As the world moves towards the information society, the correlation between truthful and easily accessible information and a higher level of exercise of rights becomes more evident. Although this relationship may not be obvious at first glance, it will be demonstrated throughout this research that information is indispensable for the exercise of other rights. Hence, access to information is classified as an instrumental one, without ignoring its end in itself, as will be explained later on. Information empowers each individual to foresee the repercussions of a decision. In contrast,

> Injecting uncertainty is a well-known control mechanism: if a population never knows what is going to happen to it, it is unlikely to pose a serious challenge to political power (Holmes 2008, 35).

That is why information becomes an element of the effective exercise of their ability to act according to their intimate convictions, and is inextricably linked to fundamental freedoms. In the absence of information, an individual becomes blind and in such a scenario, will eventually surrender his or her *freedom of choice* to whoever possesses the truth of the facts and has the authority to make decisions on behalf of others. This implies that each individual will see their own desires and interests substituted in favor of the entity or person who holds the power and the control of the information. No relinquishment of such powers can be considered deliberate if the person is not truly aware of the conditions and consequences of such a relinquishment. To put it simply: a citizen who is unaware of the effects and options on a given public decision will be practically obliged to let others – politicians, public authorities, corporations– make the decisions that affect him or her without having any say in it.

Whoever obtains information obtains power and control. The dynamics of information makes certain entities more likely to obtain and use such information: the press, academia and the state are, in fact, producers and compilers of information par excellence. This may involve public or private entities associated with information. But when the holder of information is vested with public authority, while, on the other hand, is acting in representation of others (the people), it is essential to regulate the activities it will carry out with the information it holds. It's a simple matter of regulating a potential but very likely-to-happen conflict of interests. As a result, in contemporary society, it is necessary that *access to public information* be understood as a fundamental human right derived from human freedom and dignity. Particularly in situations related to health and the environment, where timely and accurate information is needed for government officials and members of civil society to make informed decisions, information can be the deciding factor even between life and death for specific individuals under certain circumstances.

As stated above, information becomes indispensable for the exercise of, or access to, other fundamental rights or to activate their defense mechanisms. Hence the importance of having an open information system that guarantees, among other things, the quality and veracity of the information that will be made available to citizens. Likewise, the state must guarantee a solid institutional structure that promotes and protects this right effectively, as is the case with other transcendental rights. This is particularly evident in the protection of the environment, where the right of access to information is developed through a conglomerate of international treaties and declarations that have elevated this issue to the highest level, bringing the discussion to government representatives. In the European rights protection circuit, for example, the Aarhus Convention is a binding instrument that articulates the right of individuals to access environmental information and to be part of decision-making processes wherever human health or ecosystems may be at stake. The Convention also promotes access to environmental justice, i.e., the right of citizens to bring disputes involving the environment and public health to court. Similarly, in the Inter-American circuit, the Escazú Agreement is playing an increasingly relevant role in the democratization of decisions that impact the environment, productivity and development, not only in this but foreseeing consequences for future generations. Often, the tensions that arise around projects with high environmental impact generate disputes between state, corporate and citizen power. While *the law* is not the only way to bridge differences and produce solutions, states have certainly set themselves the task of generating binding instruments, both internationally and domestically, to regulate these relationships. In this context, access to environmental information has been one of the strong points of environmental regulations in general. This is a good example of how the world is moving towards a culture of public transparency and participation, at least in theory or as a *matter of course*. This places the burden on governments to ensure the production and dissemination of information and even involves private parties with an interest in the exploitation of a country's natural resources. The Inter-American Court of Human Rights ("IACrtHR") explained this relationship in the following terms:

> (...) the actions of the State must be governed by the principles of publicity and transparency in public management, which makes it possible for the people under its jurisdiction to exercise democratic control over the State's management, so that they can question, inquire and consider whether the State is adequately fulfilling its public functions. Access to information

> under the control of the State, which is of public interest, can allow participation in public management, through the social control that can be exercised with such access (Claude Reyes and Others v. Chile 2006, 46).

Not all information falls within the legal framework requiring it to be made available to the public. Information held by the state, or held by private parties on its behalf, must be accessible to the people. Cases of confidentiality and reserve are excepted, provided that such information has been expressly and previously classified, and that the classification protects the public interest and is carried out within the legal framework. All regional human rights systems have rules that regulate the handling of classified material, which should be considered as an exception to the rule of publicity (or *maximum disclosure*, as coined by the Inter-American Circuit). But this right is not limited to the possibility of requesting information and having it delivered. It is also mandatory that the information be provided with certain minimum characteristics that make it useful to citizens, in general terms, regardless of the purpose for which it is intended. This may seem a real challenge since the purpose of *seeking* information is subjective, while the standards for the dissemination of public information are objective and normative. These characteristics include truthfulness, clarity, updating of data, free of charge, among others, which will be further analyzed in the following chapters.

The concept of *public information* for its treatment as a fundamental right has developed over time and, as mentioned above, is based on the recognition of the freedom of expression (therefore classically associated with journalism), which encompasses several other prerogatives such as the possibility of seeking information, disseminating it and accessing its source. For example, the Ecuadorian Constitution[2] includes several rights related to information in the same article, including the possibility of accessing it:

- To seek.
- To receive.
- To produce.

---

[2] Article 18.- Every person, individually or collectively, has the right to:

1. Seek, receive, exchange, produce and disseminate truthful, verified, timely, contextualized, plural, uncensored information on facts, events and processes of general interest, and with the consequent responsibility.

2. Free access to information generated in public entities, or in private entities that handle State funds or perform public functions. There shall be no confidentiality of information except in cases expressly established by law. In case of violation of human rights, no public entity may deny information.

- To reach for the information generated by public entities or with state funds, free of charge.

This Constitution is one of the most comprehensive, covering several forms of exercise of this right. Having these rights recognized at the highest juridical –national Constitutions and supranational treaties– level is no minor conquest.

Without claiming to provide definitive or complete solutions, the regulations seek to guarantee a series of minimum parameters that prevent arbitrariness on the part of public officials. This is highly relevant since the information enables public scrutiny, so keeping minimum rules that facilitate the delivery could avoid systematic blockages by those officers who will, in turn, be the focus of public opinion.

However, compliance with the obligations deriving from the right of access to public information requires the fulfillment of formal and material obligations on the part of the state. The recognition of the legal right of peoples to public information implies that the norms of human rights in general, and of civil and political rights in particular, are materially applicable. Consequently, states are obliged to respect, protect, guarantee and promote this right (historically immersed within the freedom of expression or opinion), which, in most human rights catalogs, includes the right to *seek* information. Therefore, the standards of freedom of expression are also applicable to the right of access to public information: the prohibition of prior censorship and subject to subsequent accountability.

The following chapters will further analyze the limits of the concept of public information. For now, it is important to bear in mind that the right of access to public information does not necessarily overlap with private interests in which data may be subject to commercialization (provided that its commercialization is permitted by law) or involve a transcendental value for a business, especially if it is kept secret, as is the case with formulas, recipes, application models and others. Access to public information also does not interfere with personal data, which has specific regulations based on the recognition of the right to privacy, which is also a human right. As such, information is *deliverable* when it is held by public and private entities that provide public services or act on behalf of the state or state institutions, state-owned companies, federal and local governments *and* that does not conflict with other human rights. Having been produced with public funds and by mandate of the law, it is the property of the citizenry in accordance with international human rights treaties and the doctrine on the subject. Every other piece of information or data exceeds the scope of application of this right and, consequently, is not deemed deliverable to the public.

The key element is that the production of information in the administrative context is made possible through state resources (including funding, but not limited to it) and is intended to meet the needs and requirements of the population in a democratic society. Therefore, the state and its officials, as administrators of the *res publica*, are mere possessors of such information and hold it on behalf of the people as per the basic principle of democracy: power resides in the *people; information is power*. The legislations of numerous countries have developed this right through legal parameters to guarantee the prompt delivery of data and reducing restrictions to the minimum necessary. As Rojo (2010) explains, a government that promotes access to information is axiomatically aligned with the basic values of democracy:

> (...) Those who abide by the generalization of cultural conditions where the quality of democracy is a primordial value must pay special attention to the unrestricted exercise of access to timely and sufficient information by every human being and who are fully aware that the slightest violation of this right is, at the very least, a very serious situation with multiple and dire consequences (Rojo 2010, 42-43).

However, individual rights are not the only issue at stake when it comes to public information. Democracy, transparency and accountability functionally depend on the public's ability to understand the actions of their representatives, and whether they are aligned with the values of their constituents (not only the voters, but of the population in its entirety). This verification can be achieved in various ways, but there are two that prove to lead directly to the objective: firstly, the exposure of the people to the management of public resources by state officials (which implies an active role of those officials in producing information and making it available to citizens[3]) and, secondly, the ability of civil society to require information of their particular interest, assimilate it and act (or react) on the basis that it provides. Both ways of obtaining information are covered by the right of access to public information. That is to say, the citizenry can play an active role in seeking information, investigating, requesting and demanding that it be delivered to them. But even if they don't, the laws provide that certain minimum information, which is of interest to the population, is disseminated in such a way that the citizenry possesses it even without requesting it in

[3] In the context of this study, the terms "citizen" and "citizenship" do not imply the political connection of a person to a territory, but rather a person entitled to fundamental rights in a specific context, regardless of nationality, i.e., a *person* entitled to rights and obligations.

order to benefit from it even at a potential level, something like *the dew that showers the garden every morning*.

The right to petition (recognized as an independent political right in certain legal frameworks, such as Ecuador's), on the one hand, and the right to an efficient, effective and transparent public administration, on the other, also provide for access to information produced –or to be produced– in official entities. Accountability depends to a large extent on the material possibility of acquiring information that supports public activities and decisions that are relevant to the community. Thereupon, several legal standards even require that certain personal information of government authorities be known to all, such as the incoming and outgoing assets of a senior official in public office[4]. In any case, the right of access to information is supported by the obligation of the state to respond to all requests for information in a timely manner, even if it is to deny access[5].

In the Americas, the Committee on Juridical and Political Affairs of the Organization of American State ("OAS") Permanent Council appointed a group of experts, including members of civil society, to draft a model law that develops the right of access to public information and the legal principles that inform it. This model law contains the minimum standards with which states must align themselves to adequately guarantee this supra-legal right. In this model, the Commission noted the intimate relationship between access to public information, democracy and accountability. This model presents a set of important standards that are analyzed throughout this book.

Information is linked to human dignity in the sense that it is related to the right to make free decisions. Free decisions enable the exercise of the right to a good standard of living, as well as the exercise of certain political rights, including holding public authorities accountable, the transparent administration of public resources in democratic societies, the right to a healthy environment, and responsibility for the sustainability and survival of future generations. As can be seen, information covers a wide range of aspects of life in society. Concomitantly, access to public information is applicable under the principles of equality, interdependence, indivisibility and equal hierarchy of all fundamental human rights. In addition, it is necessary to take into account cross-cutting norms such as non-discrimination, gender and age-based approaches, as well as the collective rights of different minorities. In general terms, states are responsible for

[4] In some countries, including Ecuador, the obligation to disclose assets before, during and after the exercise of a public function applies to all officials of each branch of government.

[5] Del Solar 2008, 130.

ensuring that every individual is truly able to exercise the right to be informed.

The importance of this right has been explained by the United Nations ("UN") Human Rights Committee, which, once again, focuses on the importance of the availability of information and the democratic system, considering freedom of expression and opinion as *cornerstones* of freedom and democracy:

> They are the cornerstone of any free and democratic society. The two freedoms are closely related, and freedom of expression is the vehicle for the exchange and development of opinions. Freedom of expression is a necessary condition for the realization of the principles of transparency and accountability which, in turn, are essential for the promotion and protection of human rights.

This right is particularly important for the exercise and protection of certain collective rights, such as those held by ethnic minorities. The ability to acquire material information effectively leads to the possibility of exercising other rights. The International Labor Organization ("ILO") Convention 169 of 1989 on Indigenous and Tribal Peoples has become very important for involving ancestral peoples in public decisions that in some way affect their territory, culture and ways of life. Article 6 of this Convention requires that the peoples be consulted prior to the adoption of any administrative decision that may directly affect them. This means that the state has the obligation to inform them in advance and in a timely manner, as derived from the standard of good faith proclaimed therein:

> 1. In applying the provisions of this Convention, Governments shall:
> (a) Consult the peoples concerned, through appropriate procedures and in particular through their representative institutions, whenever consideration is being given to legislative or administrative measures which may affect them directly;
> (b) establish means by which these peoples can freely participate, at least to the same extent as other sectors of the population, at all levels of decision-making in elective institutions and in administrative and other bodies responsible for policies and programs which concern them;
> c) Establish the means for the full development of these peoples' own institutions and initiatives and, in appropriate cases, provide the necessary resources for this purpose.
> 2. Consultations under this Convention shall be conducted in good faith and in a form appropriate to the circumstances, with the objective of achieving agreement or consent to the proposed measures.

This essential instrument for indigenous and tribal peoples translates into the state's obligation to include these communities in any decision-making process that may affect them. Participation in the process is part of the norm, and the objective of *seeking to reach* an agreement or consensus (however subjective it may be in practice) is imposed on public actors. However, it is the principle of good faith that relates the collective right to be consulted with broad access to information regarding the decision to be made, such that even highly technical information must be didactic to ensure that the community understands the importance, benefits and risks of such a decision. This paradigm can be interpreted as a shift from representative democracy to direct democracy, in which consensus between public authorities and the people is desirable, although not mandatory. Accompanying this right, the Escazú Agreement (available to all communities at the signatory states, in the context of environmental information) establishes the parameters under which states must make information accessible to the population to enable informed decision-making. The sum of these instruments –plus a series of jurisprudential precedents on the right to be consulted– have strengthened the institution of access to information for the well-being of ancestral communities and for environmental protection.

When international instruments and local legal frameworks recognize people as owners of public information, the domain of this asset shifts from traditional actors (the state, companies, political and economic groups) to individuals and minorities. This shift of ownership is reflected in the legal bodies that generally begin with the discernment of this point: the *ownership* and *possession* of information. In the United Kingdom, the Freedom of Information Act 2000 is a rather meticulous law that recognizes the obligation of public bodies to disclose the information they hold as required by an individual, except for the statutory exemptions provided for in the same law, regulating in detail the method of accessing such data. The preamble of this norm states:

> An Act to provide for the disclosure of information held by public authorities or persons providing services to them and to amend the Data Protection Act 1998 and the Public Records Act 1958; and for connected purposes.

Another remarkable contribution of the United Kingdom government to the development of this right –as simple as it may seem– is the practicality with which it has made this norm available to the people, through an easy to navigate website, which provides an index and the different modifications of this legal norm throughout time. This implementation is not available in other countries, where the legal network is the only way to approach the norm and its mechanisms, and the exercise of this right that necessarily confronts a citizen with bureaucracy, will surely require the work of a lawyer for an effective result, which can become a barrier to exercise. On the contrary, the ease with which the norm can be understood by an ordinary citizen is an advantage for the exercise of the right.

The development of international instruments and local laws implies, not only the acknowledgement of its ownership by the people, but also a change of power dynamics over the information produced in the public sphere. This signifies a historical milestone that seems not yet to have been understood in its real dimension –as it happens when one looks closely into a fact–. Therefore, the recognition of this fundamental right by individuals is key to its wider exercise and to take advantage of its virtues by the legitimate rights holders: the citizens. This shift in power dynamics challenges traditional structures and forces a reevaluation of the balance between individual rights and societal interests. It is crucial for individuals to be aware of their rights in order to actively participate in shaping the future of information governance.

Lack of access to relevant information generates an environment of distrust in the authority. People feel insecure about the decisions they must make in a context governed by a legal framework that is generally perceived as sophisticated, intricate and alien. As a result, individuals distrust the system and its administrators, and a gradual loss of confidence in public administration is triggered. This sense of uncertainty is at least partially the result of the lack of availability of quality and sufficient public information. Usually, the less transparent systems present, at the same time, other factors that generate uncertainty, such as high levels of corruption, social inequality, authoritarianism, and others. If we add up the facts and cases, we can see how the absence or poor availability of information can contribute decisively to social chaos, in which the obscurity and ambiguity of the legal climate hinder a true rule of law because uncertainty is incompatible with a democratic structure. On the contrary, "*access to public information is the backbone of transparency*"[6]. This means that transparency is important, not only for civil society, but also for strengthening the legal capacities of political actors: authorities and law enforcement officials, who may encounter less resistance in their interactions with citizens when the latter are well informed. Public policies and guidelines to improve the culture of transparency, fight corruption and optimize citizens' access to public information, we insist, are closely related to a higher level of democracy and justice. This criterion has also been developed by Tanzi (2008) who analyzed the relationship between transparency and corruption, concluding that discretionality and lack of controls encourage corruption because it

[6] Del Solar 2008, 95.

relies on secrecy to operate. The author even provides examples of activities of authorities, with important economic effects, which deserve to be known and scrutinized by the citizens:

> There are other decisions where the discretion given to a public official, in particular, combined with the value that such decisions have for the beneficiaries of such decisions, create conditions that, in the absence of effective controls, often lead to acts of corruption. (...)
>
> Today these include (a) Decisions made by public officials in the case of legal land use, in accordance with zoning laws. Hello in these cases. Officials have the power to determine when a given piece of land can be designated for uses of low comma value, such as agriculture, or can be designated for residential use or high-rise apartments. Obviously, legal classification can dramatically change the market value of a given piece of land; (b) resolutions authorizing investments by foreign companies; (c) decisions on the sale of public assets; (d) resolutions granting monopoly powers over specific activities, such as the importation of medicines to certain individuals; (e) decisions granting amnesty to individuals or companies for obvious violations of laws; (f) determinations by which banks may receive on deposit funds from pension funds, public companies, ministries or other public institutions. There is empirical evidence that governments often leave large deposits in non-interest bearing accounts. This implies a large subsidy for the financial institutions that hold these funds. The value of these decisions, often made for private agents, can be very high, which can lead to the temptation of illegal payments.

In 2009, the Special Rapporteur appointed by the Human Rights Council, Frank La Rue, mentioned the intrinsic connection between corruption and secrecy, and advocated the observance of the principle of maximum disclosure, which allows "*governments and public institutions* to *be more accountable to the public at large*". As part of his conclusions and recommendations, he stated:

> Governments may not be in a position to systematically disseminate information to the public or may not be inclined to such transparency due to high levels of corruption. The Special Rapporteur recommends that, in such cases, support for media in times of conflict and deregulation of the communications and media environment be considered as mechanisms to increase plurality and diversity of information flows in poor and conflict-prone countries. (United Nations Human Rights Council, 2009).

However, the mere establishment of public policies on transparency is insufficient to achieve the highest possible level of transparency nor of exercise of human rights. Effectiveness requires educating people about the *ownership* of public data; it is essential to implant this notion among the population and to achieve the political commitment it entails. Training is of utmost importance for this purpose. To this day, despite decades of development of the right of access to public information in the legal scenario, the general population is not aware of its right. Not only members of civil society, but also public officials who are subject to a set of rules and obligations relating to this right are trapped in a system of access that, in a large number of countries, is still alien to them. In general terms, this system is composed of guidelines, proactive duties of disclosure, specialized institutions and officials, as well as specific complaint mechanisms and sanction regimes that can even lead to the removal from office of those obliged subjects who fail to comply with the duty to inform and provide information. This implies serious challenges for the fulfillment of the obligations derived from this right and from the international instruments that contemplate them.

The above is also interrelated with the institutional strategic objectives of the entities with the role of monitoring the level of execution of the obligations derived from the right. In some countries, this duty falls to specialized entities exclusively in charge of the right to information (see, for example, Mexico's National Transparency Institute, in charge of monitoring compliance with its respective transparency and personal data protection legislation). In other countries, this is one of the many tasks of the Ombudsman or national human rights institutions (as in Ecuador, where the Ombudsman is the legal supervisor of compliance with the obligations of state entities in relation to transparency, but also on other human rights). This is an uphill struggle if one takes into account the hundreds of central government institutions, decentralized, autonomous, federal or local governments (depending on the political structure of each country) and entities of other branches, including state-owned enterprises, which are subject to similar transparency standards. To this end, various methods are implemented, such as monitoring programs, publication schemes and templates, and periodic reporting systems. However, according to the models implemented in certain countries, the state oversight and control agency must be specialized in the subject in order to give life to the standard and, therefore, to the right of access to public information. The subject to be monitored is too broad for a generic institution to handle it on its own.

Another important issue is funding. Since state bodies will be subject to the control of this Ombudsman (specialized or generic), the tendency is to maintain a reduced budget for them, especially in countries where the level of transparency and respect for human rights is lower, which are generally also the countries with lower democratic standards… and diminished public resources. In the United Kingdom, the public body responsible for overseeing this right is the Information Commissioner's Office ("ICO"), sponsored by the Department of Science, Innovation and Technology, which reports to the English Parliament. Its mission is to "*uphold information rights in the public interest, promoting openness of public bodies and data privacy for individuals*"[7]. According to its website, it is funded almost entirely by the data protection levy required of bodies handling personal data. The ICO is responsible for the protection of private data and the dissemination of public information and makes available different resources for both purposes.

As a corollary, the higher the levels of public information dissemination, the higher the democratic standards. A government's openness in this regard is a good symptom of its commitment to democracy and the fight against corruption. On the contrary, the tendency to withhold information –either to protect certain privileged interests or to avoid public control–, is a symptom of an unreliable resource management. The legitimacy of political authority today depends to a large extent on the provision of quality data. There is no loss of power when important information is shared in a healthy democracy and egalitarian society: when information is available, everyone wins. But this idea raises two major hurdles to overcome: public cost and political tensions.

The State and the right of access to public information

The purpose of the *principle of publicity* in public administration is to guarantee transparent, reliable processes, respectful of legal and ethical standards in the management of public resources. It does not only cover economic resources, but all those that, due to their social relevance, become resources of public interest because they can massively affect various aspects of the life of society. This includes information management, which is an important public resource. According to Fernández (2006, 149), the principle of publicity consists of the transparency with which governments must act, make decisions and undertake procedures, being agents of the law at the service of the people. In the author's words, this principle implies:

> ... that the acts of the agencies of the State, the grounds on which they are based and the procedures according to which they are adopted are notorious, patent or manifest and not secret, reserved, hidden or concealed, that is, that any person may have access to such information as a result of which, in the

[7] Information Commissioner's Office "ICO", 2023.

> Democratic and Constitutional Rule of Law, it must always act with transparency that allows and promotes that the people know those acts, their foundations and the procedures followed to adopt them.

Therefore, in case of doubt, the authorities must opt for access to information and comply with the state's duty to promote the rights enshrined in international human rights treaties that are adopted in the exercise of each country's sovereignty. And, if there are no other human rights in collision with a specific request for access to information (as may be the case of secrecy of correspondence, personal beliefs, personal data, national security or others), state officials are obliged to provide the information in accordance with the legal standards established by the legislation of each country. This means that the principle of publicity articulates freedom of information, embodied in the right of everyone to access public information. This is known as the principle of maximum disclosure, a standard that establishes a presumption of publicity of information in favor of its release.

The state is responsible for promoting, guaranteeing and respecting the right of access to public information, as mentioned above. The right to information requires more than communicating acts of public power; it involves printing transparency in the decisions of government authorities and facilitating their recognition by the population (Lavalle Cobo, 2009). Even more: for modern democracies, the active participation of the population in the adoption of public decisions has become a democratic standard. The mechanisms of direct democracy are enabled through the provision of timely information for a real participation of the population. To this end, domestic and international law have established a series of instruments that bind governments and oblige them to carry out certain activities and to refrain from others that impede the enjoyment and exercise of this right. The consensus on a regime of exceptions also derives from these instruments, considering them acceptable to the extent that they serve the general interest, i.e., the protection and defense of the interests represented by the high values of the international instruments and constitutional law in each country. This reflects that the right of access to information is under a higher level of protection. In sum, what the state must guarantee is greater access to information that promotes a culture of transparency as opposed to the secrecy of public administration, and that allows for greater public scrutiny, informed decisions by citizens, legal certainty and the full application of the democratic principle, since uncertainty that is built on improper information or rumors prevents timely and true political participation.

The right to information is an unfinished institution due to its character as a social and historical fact that guarantees its constant evolution and dynamism. Likewise, it is impossible to claim a homogeneous application in the different countries of the planet –culturally, there is not even uniformity within countries–. However, the norms must aim at equal treatment, considering that each state has its own social, political and legal characteristics, but that the right to equality is transversal. Therefore, since it is recognized as a right derived from human dignity, it must have specific characteristics that allow its universal exercise by individuals and groups throughout the world.

Returning to the conceptualization of information as an asset, its categorization must be meticulously considered to avoid conflicts with private interests that may impede collective access. A parallel can be drawn with other basic goods that were once in the hands of the public and today, due to the transformation of the way of life and the economic pressures that this implies, people's ability to appropriate such goods has been reduced. Water, wind and sunlight are concepts that were historically understood as public domain goods. Traditionally, it is taught in schools that these elements are *free goods* of humanity. However, the privatization of water sources and the production of energy through wind and sunlight have changed this concept and people are being charged for the transformation that allows the daily use of these elements. This is the present and the future of information. Because of its importance, data appropriation is related to business activities and decisions about where or how to invest and what this means for the transformation of the way of life of communities. However, *public information* is understood as part of the public heritage and as such should be managed by governments.

The following chapters will address this issue from the perspective of international human rights law, constitutional law and the development of judicial precedents of international courts in Europe and America. Useful contributions of certain directives and legislation of the European Union and particularly of the United Kingdom are also addressed, without leaving aside the casuistry on the subject. In addition, this study will be supported by developments in the following Latin American countries that present some interesting developments: Argentina, Ecuador and Mexico. The study will focus on the jurisprudence of these regions, since, to a large extent, it is through the jurisdictional bodies with supranational competence that the elements of this fundamental right have developed, that is, through the practice of law and the interaction between governments, journalists, human rights defenders and ordinary citizens.

INFORMATION IN THE CONTEXT OF FUNDAMENTAL RIGHTS

Historical recognition

The scope and content of the right of access to public information is a recent development compared to other political rights. It is associated with freedom of the press and opinion, and although this has been an important anchor for its recognition as a fundamental right, it has been emerging as a right in its own, interdependent but with its own characteristics. Access to information *was* not *born* at some point in history to endow human beings with a new capacity. On the contrary, it is inherent to the human condition and to individual freedom, and, at the same time, it derives from the democratic and republican principles. In this sense, the fact that it is not provided for in a legal norm does not hinder its exercise, because it is part of humanity and is universal. The law only recognizes this reality and regulates its scope and limits to guarantee its enjoyment and exercise. Thus, the essence of the right of access to public information was somehow *hidden* in the freedom of opinion, as can be seen in the International Covenant on Civil and Political Rights, adopted by the General Assembly of the United Nations on December 16, 1966, whose article 19 states:

> Everyone has the right to hold opinions without interference.
> Everyone shall have the right to freedom of expression; *this right shall include freedom to seek*, receive and impart information and ideas of all kinds, regardless of frontiers, either orally, in writing or in print, in the form of art, or through any other media of his choice.
> 3. The exercise of the rights provided for in paragraph 2 of this Article entails special duties and responsibilities. It may therefore be subject to certain restrictions, but these shall only be such as are provided by law and are necessary:
> a) Out of respect for the rights or reputation of others;
> b) For the protection of national security or of public order, or of public health or morals.

Montero (2020), in her short but essential analysis of this right, gives a historical account that summarizes quite accurately the trajectory of access to information in the UN. As shown by her research, this process begun rather late compared to the development of freedom of expression.

> Special mention should be made of the role of the UN Commission on Human Rights in creating, in 1993, the Special Rapporteur on Freedom of Opinion and Expression (Resolution 1993/45 of March 5, 1993), which in 1998 published a report in which it noted "the positive obligation of States to ensure access to information, particularly with respect to information held by the Government" (Report of the Special Rapporteur on the promotion and protection of the right to freedom of opinion and expression. U.N. DOC. Doc. E/CN. 4/1998/40, 28 January 1998). Similarly, but taking a leap forward, the 2000 report qualified, for the first time, access to information as a "fundamental right" (Report of the Special Rapporteur on the promotion and protection of the right to freedom of opinion and expression. U.N. DOC. Doc. E/CN. 4/2000/63, 18 January 2000).

Access to information was not considered a subjective right for a long time. In Europe, this condition was evident and, given the existence of internal and community rules that promoted secrecy, access permission was considered to be a "*matter of internal organization*"[8], practically a rule of administrative orderliness. In this regard, there is an extensive debate in the Court of Justice of the European Community, in the case of the Netherlands v. Council of the European Union (cited by Rams Ramos 2008). There, the Netherlands argued that the right of access comes from and *is* the realization of the democratic principle and that, thus understood, it does not require a norm that positivizes it. It took many years for the right of access to be configured as such and to be implemented through norms that provide specific obligations to the states of the Union.

Article 10 of the European Convention on Human Rights guarantees freedom of expression, developed through the case law of the European Court of Human Rights ("ECrtHR"), which has stated that it includes the right to *receive* information and ideas.

> Freedom of expression
> Everyone has the right to freedom of expression. This right shall include freedom to hold opinions and to *receive and impart information and ideas* without interference by public authority and regardless of frontiers. This article shall not prevent States from requiring the licensing of broadcasting, television, or motion picture enterprises.
> 2. The exercise of these freedoms, insofar as it carries with it duties and responsibilities, may be subject to such formalities, conditions, restrictions or penalties as are prescribed by law and are necessary in a democratic

[8] Rams Ramos 2008, 86.

> society in the interests of national security, territorial integrity or public safety, for the prevention of disorder or crime, for the protection of health or morals, for the protection of the reputation or rights of others, for preventing the disclosure of confidential information, or for maintaining the authority and impartiality of the judiciary.

UNESCO, in its comprehensive study of the legal standards for the freedom of expression and access to information, considers that freedom of expression is integrated by the legal feasibility of *seeking* information and disseminating it, which contemplates the same guarantees as the right to express an opinion. To seek information will necessarily ensure access to public sources. In other words, the production of ideas and their communication to others would be truncated if the search for information is restricted or limited because that restricted information will feed the opinion to be disseminated. Therefore, in order to form an opinion, it is only natural to have access to information gathered or produced of others in the first place. This is not to deny the possibility of a spontaneous and creative production of ideas, but there is nothing new under the sun: as a general rule, knowledge is based on something that existed previously.

> Thus, there are three principles at the core of the right to freedom of expression:
> - The right to hold opinions without interference;
> - The right to seek and receive information;
> - The right to disseminate information of any kind by any means, regardless of frontiers UNESCO (2021, 23).

Without dismissing the interdependence between the right of access to information and the fundamental freedom to form and express an opinion, provided for in the aforementioned continental and international instruments, it is essential to recognize the nature of this right as a prerogative in itself that will not necessarily be exercised in consonance with those or other rights[9]. In simple terms, the right of access to public information is a right in itself, and this, today, is undeniable, having achieved supranational legal recognition and legislative and jurisprudential development in most countries.

Within the European region, the recognition of the right of access to public information experienced a nuanced trajectory, culminating in its

[9] Often, the right of access to public information is the prelude to the exercise of other fundamental rights, since it has an instrumental facet. Therefore, it must be recognized in its dimensions of right-means and right-ends that complement each other.

formal recognition by the European Parliament and, more broadly, in the paradigmatic transition from a culture of secrecy, characterized by strict restrictions on disclosure, to a code emphasizing maximum publicity. This was not only an administrative practice; secrecy of information was the norm and dissemination the exception. According to Rams Ramos (2008), before the 1980s, making an administrative document available to the public was rare as secrecy was mandatory.

> (...) access to the writings contained in historical archives was only recognized, and only after thirty years from their production, until the current definition given by Regulation No. 1049-2001. (...)
>
> Until the 1990s, when the Member States took into account the need to establish a system of access to documents and information held by the European institutions - with the approval of the Maastricth Treaty and, above all, due to the problems of its ratification and, subsequently, of the Amsterdam Treaty (...)
>
> It is mainly the strength of Member States with a tradition of openness – such as Sweden, Denmark, the Netherlands and Finland – that gave a definite impetus to the development and recognition of the right of access. (Rams Ramos, 2008, 74-75).

In 2001, the European Parliament enacted Regulation No. 1049/2001 regarding public access to European Parliament, Council and Commission documents. The Regulation entitles any citizen or resident of the European Union to access those documents produced by that supranational legislative body, under a regime of exceptions that take into account public interests and private rights, including commercial protection. Its issuance achieved, at a high level, people's access to documents held or produced by those organisms. A true change of paradigm.

Relying on the European Convention on Human Rights, in 1996 the ECrtHR ruled on a case in which a United Kingdom judge required a journalist to disclose a source who had shared information about a local company's business plan. Through this judgment (and other similar ones), the European Court confirmed that "*freedom of expression constitutes one of the essential foundations of a democratic society and that the guarantees to be afforded to the press are of particular importance.*" Moreover, the protection of journalists and their sources to ensure an informed society is part of the obligations of the contracting states under the European Convention. Consequently, avoiding harassment of media workers and their informants becomes a negative obligation of all public authorities, and the Court explains why:

> The applicant and the Commission were of the view that Article 10 of the Convention required that any obligation imposed on a journalist to disclose his or her source should be limited to exceptional circumstances where vital public or individual interests were at stake (...) In any event, the degree of public interest in the information could not be a test of whether there was a pressing social need to order disclosure of the source. A source may provide information of little value one day and of great value the next; what mattered was that the relationship between the journalist and the source generated the kind of information that had legitimate newsworthiness potential. (Goodwin v. United Kingdom, 1996).

Similarly, in one of the landmark cases on the protection of the right to information (Társaság a Szabadságjogokért (TASZ) v. Hungary 2005), the ECrtHR stated that the protection of the press in the search for the truth was a matter of public interest and therefore subject to a higher level of scrutiny when imposing barriers by representatives of the state:

> In any event, the Court notes that "the right to freedom to receive information basically prohibits a Government from restricting a person from receiving information that others wish or may be willing to impart to him" (*Leander*, *op. cit.*, § 74). It considers that the present case essentially concerns an interference – by virtue of the censorial power of an information monopoly – with the exercise of the functions of a social watchdog, like the press, rather than a denial of a general right of access to official documents. In this connection, a comparison can be drawn with the Court's previous concerns that preliminary obstacles created by the authorities in the way of press functions call for the most careful scrutiny.

The cited case became a milestone for the protection of this right in the region. But the case also demonstrates the tension between the state and the citizenry in advancing the battle line for their own interests. The conflict concerned a denial of access by the Hungarian Constitutional Court, later upheld by the Budapest Regional Court, to a constitutional file, despite having a law allowing access to information, the "Protection of Personal Data and the Public Nature of Data of Public Interest". The state argued that the requested file was not considered *public data under* the aforementioned law. At that time, the ECtHR struggled with the concept of open access to administrative information, and was able to set a precedent in this regard:

> The Court recalls at the outset that "Article 10 does not ... confer on the individual a right of access to a register containing information on his personal position, nor does it embody an obligation on the Government to impart such information to the individual" (*Leander v. Sweden*, 26 March 1987, § 74 *in fine*, Series A no. 116) and that "it is difficult to derive from

> the Convention a general right of access to administrative data and documents" (*Loiseau v. France* (dec.), no. 46809/99, ECHR 2003-XII (extracts)). Nevertheless, the Court has recently advanced towards a broader interpretation of the notion of "freedom to receive information" (see *Sdružení Jihočeské Matky c. la République tchèque* (dec.), no. 19101/03, 10 July 2006) and thereby towards the recognition of a right of access to information.

These cases manifest how access to public information was first understood as a necessity for the profession of journalism and broadcasting, at a time when the population was informed mainly through newspapers and traditional media. However, journalists have not been conceived as holders of this right, notwithstanding that their work is of interest to the entire population. In this sense, although they were the spearhead for this right to obtain its form and recognition as a prerogative of the freedom of expression, it is widely understood that the holders of rights relating to information as a common good, as well as the owners of the same, is the public –this configuration is present in most of the current legislation in democratic countries–.

The IACrtHR has not neglected the analysis of this right either, although it is far from being exhausted. In 2006, through Claude Reyes v. Chile, the Court outlined the main standards in the different cases it had heard up to that time, which are binding for the contracting states of the Inter-American Convention on Human Rights. Latin America bears now the challenge of following the path traced through the development of this high court's case law. The next step is to overcome the limitations to the realization of the norms in the same way as has been done with other fundamental rights –a task in progress, undoubtedly. In this context, these standards should be considered guidelines for the design of domestic legislation and public policies. In the area of transparency, accountability and access to public information, the reticence of officials and authorities may be more profound than in the case of other fundamental rights, as it reveals their acts and omissions and holds them accountable for any undesired results. According to these standards, the right to obtain information, as the very core of the right of access to public information, implies positive and negative obligations on the part of the public administrations.

The importance of these precedents developed by the supranational Courts, as well as by the American and the European Commissions of Human Rights, highlight the states' obligation to respect this right and remove obstacles to its full exercise (or to reach the highest possible level of such).

Giving shape to this obligation has not been an easy task for supranational courts or for states. It has been a long way for the European and Inter-American Courts to outline a definition of the core of this fundamental right through their jurisprudence, considering that the right of access to public information was not originally conceived as an autonomous right in the respective catalogs. In the Inter-American circuit, Claude Reyes et. al. v. Chile (2006) is, even today, the most prominent precedent of the IACrtHR on this issue. UNESCO (2021, 82) recognized that this circuit has *"a clearer and stronger jurisprudence"* and cites this case to portray the fundamental pillars of the right of access public information. This controversy was about a group of researchers who demanded that the Republic of Chile turn over information about an investment agreement between private parties that was authorized by a government agency. Some of the information was withheld due to its private (commercial) nature; however, the Court declared that such withholding was illegal:

> The Tribunal finds it clear that the information that was not provided by the State was of public interest, as it related to a foreign investment contract originally entered into between the State and two foreign companies and a Chilean recipient company for the purpose of developing a forestry industrialization project, which, due to its potential environmental impact, generated a great deal of public discussion. (Claude Reyes et al. v. Chile 2006, 42).

The relevance of this judgment lies in the characterization of the right of access to public information, clarifying its status as a human right and developing the standards to be observed by countries that adhere to the American Convention on Human Rights. Moreover, the Court highlighted some aspects that constitute a real advance in the field of human rights:

- The right of access to public information is part of the right to freedom of thought and expression (Article 13 of the Convention).
- The recognition of the right to seek information implies that each state must (i) respect this right, (ii) guarantee it and (iii) adopt provisions of domestic law to make it effective.
- The quality of information as public –or not– is given by the importance it has for the community, which means that it should not be withheld if it is considered to be of public interest.
- Restrictions on this right may only be imposed by a legal instrument, not by inferior legislation or by particular

administrative acts or decisions. Additionally, restrictions must serve a purpose permitted by the Convention, such as public order, national security or respect for other fundamental rights.

- The principle of maximum disclosure is combined with the principle of necessity, which means that the least restrictive option for the protection of conflicting interests must be adopted in all cases.

Following the path of international circuits for the protection of human rights, domestic legislations have included the right or access either as part of the freedom of expression or freedom of thought, or as an independent right. The Mexican National Constitution follows this trend and, in recognizing freedom of opinion, includes the right to information as a guarantee of the state, which is understood to be subject to the same limits that are upheld in this article (limits that will be analyzed later on):

> Article 6
> The expression of ideas shall not be subject to any judicial or administrative inquisition, except in the case that it violates morals, the rights of third parties, provokes a crime or disturbs public order; the right to information shall be guaranteed by the State.

As such, this fundamental freedom includes, from the beginning of its recognition in modern Western legal history, the right to seek information. The right of access to information produced by the state has been built from this extract, which was understood by the representatives of the countries in the General Assembly of the United Nations as a natural component of the right to express an opinion. It is necessary to insist: how could a human being compose his or her own opinion on any matter, without information to feed it?

But the construction of this right has other important milestones. On June 18, 2009, the Council of Europe adopted the Convention on Access to Official Documents (the Tromso Convention), which remains open for signature by member states and accession by non-member states and any international organization. The Convention recently entered into force upon its tenth ratification by Ukraine on December 1, 2020. The importance of this instrument is radical in the consolidation of the right of access to public information as a right inherent to democracy. Its contributions to the institutional framework are unquestionable and will be reviewed later, but for now, it is worth mentioning that Article 1 provides for the disclosure of information as a general rule, while establishing a list of possible legitimate grounds for limiting access in the countries party to the Convention (Article

3). The allowed limitations, once again, include national security, public safety, legitimate private interests and commercial interests, among others.

In the field of environmental protection, several strong instruments have been developed to make access to public information effective and to enable decision-making procedures that include communities when it comes to projects or activities that affect the environment, safety and health. On June 25, 1998, the United Nations Economic Commission for Europe adopted the Convention on Access to Information, Public Participation in Decision-making and Access to Justice in Environmental Matters (the "Aarhus Convention"), which entered into force on October 30, 2001. In addition to creating pollution inventories for industrial activities and making them accessible to the public, it develops standards for access to and use of information to enable and encourage public participation in plans, programs, policy-making activities and legislation.

Meanwhile, in the Americas, the Regional Agreement on Access to Information, Public Participation and Access to Justice in Environmental Matters in Latin America and the Caribbean (the "Escazú Agreement") represents an important step forward on the matter. Adopted on March 4, 2018 and entering into force in 2021, it addresses the need of communities, particularly human rights defenders, to access quality information on projects and activities that may impact the environment, as well as the right to participate in such decision-making processes and the right to access justice in environmental matters. In addition, this agreement takes into account the importance of territory for indigenous peoples and other ethnic groups, thus ensuring special conditions to guarantee their material access to relevant information. The Agreement imposes on states the obligation to report in the following terms:

> Article 5
> Access to environmental information
> *Accessibility of environmental information*
> Each Party shall ensure the public's right of access to environmental information in its possession, control or custody, in accordance with the principle of maximum disclosure.
> 2. The exercise of the right of access to environmental information includes:
> a) *request and receive information* from the competent authorities without mentioning any special interest or explaining the reasons for the request;
> b) *be informed promptly* whether or not the information requested is in the possession of the competent authority receiving the request, and
> c) *To be informed of the right to challenge* and appeal when information is not provided, as well as the requirements to exercise it.
> 3. Each Party shall facilitate access to environmental information to persons or groups in vulnerable situations, establishing procedures for the provision

> of assistance, from the formulation of requests to the delivery of information, taking into account their conditions and specificities, in order to promote equal access and participation.
> 4. Each Party shall ensure that the above-mentioned vulnerable individuals or groups, including indigenous peoples and ethnic groups, receive assistance in preparing their requests and obtaining a response.

As the most recent international treaty on the subject in the Americas, it has a high academic relevance along with its legal and social importance. As will be discussed below, the standards recognized in Article 5 of the Escazú Agreement involve the different approaches that have been developed towards this right over time, providing for more equitable relations between the state and civil society in the scope of its applicability.

This right has several levels that must be observed by the state and other obligated subjects, since only by verifying compliance with each one of them in specific cases can we speak of a real exercise of this right. Both in international law and in domestic public law, access to information comprises formal and material elements that must necessarily be verified cumulatively so that the state, in the person of whoever holds public power at the given time, can fulfill its responsibility.

Information Law and Human Rights

Information law is a branch of public law that studies the fundamental right of people to be informed. Why is this important? Because by locating the legal branch to which this right belongs, it will be easier to understand its nature, development and substantial elements. The particular features that the juridical study provides allow for its delimitation; it is just as locating an address in a large neighborhood.

The subjective right to information, whose holders are all persons, is the object of study of this branch of law. Mexican jurist Perla Gómez (2011) refers to this right as a fundamental *and* human right. Likewise, the Inter-American Law Model on Access to Information (2010), developed by a group of experts commissioned by the OAS, uses this double term. This entails that access to information derives from human dignity, equality and freedom; meanwhile, it is essential for the structure of states, for democracy and for the concept of self-determined societies.

Thus, this right, of a human-fundamental nature, includes the prerogatives of gathering information, the right to inform and the right to be informed. It has been developed as such through various international instruments, such as the Universal Declaration of Human Rights, the International Covenant on Civil and Political Rights and the American Convention on Human

Rights. In none of these instruments will the "right of access to public information" be found explicitly, but each of them contains freedom of expression or opinion, which, in turn, describe these powers. The European Convention on Human Rights, for its part, does not include the right to *seek* information as part of freedom of expression, and only holds the right to inform and be informed. This relationship can be described as concentric circles: information law holds within it the right to information; inside it we find freedom of expression; and from freedom of expression derives the right to have authentic data kept in public databases that will become public information, and also the right of access to such public information.

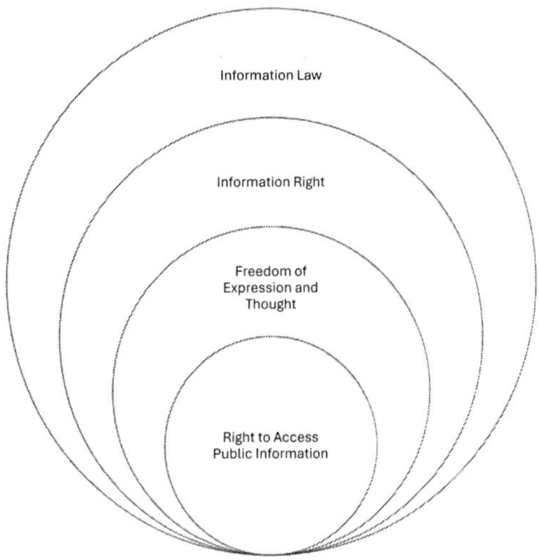

This does not entail some type of hierarchy among these rights; it merely poses the instrumentation of the right of access as it has been developed through legal bodies. It is important to stress that all human rights are of the same hierarchy.

Now, every human right has three main elements that define it. These are the subject, the object and the faculties involved in its recognition. Within the faculties there are irreducible minimum standards that constitute its hard core and that, if they are undermined, a violation of the right occurs. Certain prerogatives of each right may be regulated by law, but its core must be protected at all times. This exercise can be carried out with any fundamental right to approach the logic behind this notion. The components of its core may be more comprehensible if the elements are contrasted with those of another fundamental right with which most of us are more familiar, such as the right to health, for example:

	Right to information	Right to health
Subject	Every human being, without distinction, privilege or restriction of any kind.	Every human being, without distinction, privilege or restriction of any kind.
Object	Information held by public bodies, regardless of its source.	The highest attainable standard of physical and mental health that enables a person to live with dignity.
Powers of the Subject	Right to collect information, right to inform and right to be informed.	Enjoy facilities, goods, services and conditions that allow the highest possible level of health.

In this sense, by comparing the right to information with a right chosen at random, but of the same hierarchy as the previous one –since both are fundamental to human dignity, freedom and equality– it is possible to become aware of the structure that information possesses in order to be profiled as a human right.

In this context, the right to information is indispensable for collective and individual human development, since it guarantees the role of the human being as a social and political actor, as well as several others that could be enumerated. Information is a tool for the exercise of other rights, be they political, economic, social and cultural rights, or diffuse rights such as the right to a healthy environment, development or consumer rights. Access to quality information must therefore be guaranteed to all people, all the time.

The right of access to public information has two dimensions. On the one hand, it is an individual right, which consists of the power of a citizen to request information and to receive it when it is proven that it constitutes public information. On the other hand, there is the collective dimension, as a form of containment of the state apparatus, control of the actions of its officials and participation in the decisions of public power, not as an individual but as a community. But, additionally, this collective dimension is manifested in the way in which information feeds the public opinion, empowering the enjoyment of this right in a *passive way* by the public, which is informed based on the research of a third party. As determined by the Colombian Constitutional Court, cited by Villanueva (2003, XVIII), the right to information has a double and significant role, critical when defining its scope: it corresponds not only to the person who *provides* the information (active subject), but also to the persons *receiving* the information (passive subjects), both under the same international protection. In the context of a media-citizen relationship, the citizen is considered the right-holder of the right to information, being, therefore, the recipient of state protection, despite the media being the information provider. The state, in this relationship, protects the exercise of the right by establishing legal limits to regulate the media and their social duty to inform in a truthful and ethical manner, and by exercising controls that, in general, are *ex post*, so that these limits are respected. However, in the relationship between the state and the media, it is the media that have rights and guarantees that the state is obliged to respect and that determine that the authorities cannot restrict the dissemination of information by sacrificing public debate. In sum, in all cases the state is responsible for safeguarding the rights of citizens (who are also subjects of other constitutional rights) by establishing policies and regulations and effective controls to ensure that they are complied with.

The UN Human Rights Committee addressed this notion in General Comment No. 34 (2011, 1) where all the components or "sub-rights" (for a more graphic understanding) of the right to information are explained with the purpose of a consensual application by governments. In addition to the importance of public information for a highly democratic society (mentioned in previous sections of this study), this Committee brings this concept closer to the individual. The first part of the opinion states conclusively, "*Freedom of opinion and freedom of expression are indispensable conditions for the full development of the individual.*" For the Committee, the protection of those who strive for the protection and advancement of the right to information is an obligation of member states. This includes, but is not limited to, human rights defenders, environmental activists, researchers and lawyers, as well as journalists:

> Journalists are frequently subjected to such threats, intimidation and attacks because of their activities. So too are persons who engage in the gathering and analysis of information on the human rights situation and who publish human rights-related reports, including judges and lawyers. All such attacks should be vigorously investigated in a timely fashion, and the perpetrators prosecuted, and the victims, or, in the case of killings, their representatives, be in receipt of appropriate forms of redress. (...)
>
> It is not compatible with paragraph 3, for instance, to invoke such [treason and similar] laws to suppress or withhold from the public information of legitimate public interest that does not harm national security or to prosecute journalists, researchers, environmental activists, human rights defenders, or

> others, for having disseminated such information. (UN Human Rights Committee 2011, 6)

It is worth noting that the General Opinion may not be considered a finished criterion, but rather a notion of the current state of the concept of law. All fundamental rights are under the principle of progressivity and evolve together with the evolution of society in a specific period of history. Consequently, this interpretation can only be understood as a *minimum standard at the time* of its publication, and as such must be integrated in the resolution of particular cases in the courts of the countries and by the supranational circuits of protection of human rights. However, the importance of this opinion lies in its issuance by the United Nations, which encompasses 193 states bound by the Universal Declaration on Human Rights.

But it is not only journalistic work that is directly related to access to information. Human rights advocates have tirelessly sought, often at the cost of their own lives, to gain access to information about serious human rights violations, especially those resulting from war, generalized violence or dictatorships. From this quest derives another "sub-right" of the right to information: *the right to truth*. The right to the truth, coined by various legislations, including Argentina's, after its long and painful history of massive human rights violations during the dictatorship, implies the obligation to inform society and the family of the aggrieved, of the real facts and circumstances, the whereabouts of the victims or their mortal remains, as well as those responsible. The search for answers is not just about justice, but also about closure and the ability to move forward with their lives. Seeking answers and accountability for these disappearances is crucial not only for the victims and their families, but also for society as a whole in order to prevent such atrocities from happening again. It is well known that the disappearances caused by the de facto governments in Argentina and Chile (as has also occurred in various countries around the world) have disrupted the life project of a large number of people and their families, who have demanded to know in depth the facts of which they have been direct or indirect victims, beyond the possibility of criminal prosecution of these crimes. This connection underscores the importance of information for the personal life project.

According to the OAS Department for Effective Public Management, the range of aspects of daily life that are enhanced by the availability of relevant public information is quite broad. From the improvement of financial services to the security of food establishments and even to outreach to community police members, the Department shows how governments and citizens connect and achieve synergies to address common problems from an inclusive perspective, exchanging confrontation for mutual support. One of the facts that the report highlights as an achievement is the Peruvian transparency program in extractive industries, such as mining, which normally generates high tensions between government authorities, civil society, indigenous communities and private companies. Peru has diagnosed and addressed the problems that hindered the development of communities surrounding mineral extracting projects. According to the OAS brief (2013, 25), Peru was the first country to obtain a compliance certification by the International Council for Local Environmental Initiatives, due to its information management. The situation analyzed does not imply a utopian scenario in which conflict and confrontation are absolutely absent, but certainly the level of conflict is reduced by enabling informed and inclusive dialogue.

As for economic, social and cultural rights, the list of cases that could be cited to demonstrate the real need for the information produced by the government is probably endless. By way of example, in 2012, in Ecuador, a case was brought before the Ombudsman's Office regarding the human right to health, affected by the absence of regulation guaranteeing the safety of biosimilar drugs for the treatment of cancer. According to the complaint, despite the lack of regulations and, therefore, of effective controls, the drug was already being marketed in the country, which appears as a violation of the right to have safe, effective and quality drugs.[10] The core of the case was the absence of technical and transparent information that would allow doctors and patients to determine the safety of the similar biomolecular drug for the treatment of relapsed or refractory follicular lymphoma. In that case, the health surveillance institution was not withholding information but had allegedly not required it at all, nor had it issued adequate technical regulations for similar biomolecular drugs. In other words, the violation of the right occurred due to the absence of sufficient and timely information. This case demonstrates the domino effect between the violation of the right to information and other human rights due to the existing connection insofar as they affect people's quality of life.

Information is also crucial for access to justice, a fair trial and an adequate defense, all of which are guaranteed by human rights treaties and developed by international courts, especially when citizens are confronted with state acts and decisions. Such is the importance of having reliable data that several legislations have reversed the burden of proof to require government authorities under scrutiny to be the ones to provide evidence to support the legitimacy of the administrative acts in trial. The Escazú Agreement, in regulating environmental justice, provides for the reversal of

[10] DPE-DINAPROT-DESC-54059-2011-ASD, 2012.

the burden of proof and the principle of dynamic burden of proof, which requires that the entity that is in the best position to prove a fact is obliged to do so, regardless of its position in the dispute, as plaintiff or defendant.

Based on these facts, it is unquestionably concluded that information is a tool that enables the practice of other human rights. Consequently, a breach of the right to access information can have varying degrees of influence on multiple other fundamental rights. The nature of this right is dual: it exists as an autonomous right in itself, and also serves as a means for citizens to enhance their way of life, both individually and collectively.

Public Information: Building a Concept

The scope of this right is an issue that requires careful consideration. It is important to fully understand the implications and limitations of this right before making any decision, especially from the point of view of public officials who may be subject to liability –that may include criminal liability– if they allow disclosure of protected information. While the principle of "maximum disclosure" should guide the relationship between public administrators and persons requesting access, there is a strong interest in keeping certain information out of the public domain. In this manner, public officials may be bound, at the same time, by two opposable legal standards. This chapter will explore the matter of the right of access to public information and the acceptable exceptions, as well as the tests necessary to resolve cases of doubt. The criteria developed by supranational courts will reflect the way in which these issues have been resolved in the casuistry.

In the Ecuadorian legal framework, "public information" is understood as all information emanating from or held by public sector institutions (including state enterprises) or private entities which, due to the subject matter of the information, have state participation or are concessionaires of the same. It also includes all information obtained with public resources. The definition is similar to the Freedom of Information Act of the United Kingdom and, in both cases, the law poses certain limitations to the breadth of this concept. Argentina's Access to Public Information Law No. 27275 includes a legal presumption of publicity. In the case of Mexico, the Federal Law of Transparency and Access to Public Information includes several forms of possession of data that imply the publicity of information, such as the acquisition and transformation of information, in addition to its generation.

To understand the obligations arising from the recognition of the right of access to public information, it is first necessary to contextualize the right before approaching its core. As mentioned above, the object on which this right takes effect is the *obtaining* of information that is generated in the public system. The concept of *public information* is entirely complex and requires a case-by-case study under certain circumstances, particularly when there are legal assets of equal value at stake (*among others*, other fundamental rights, human security, international relations). López-Ayllón

(2003) defines the right to information as a fundamental freedom of the human being, which would confirm that the state has negative obligations towards the people or, in other words, duties of abstention. However, the right of access to public information also implies positive obligations, such as the proactive dissemination of information, the collection of documents and their reproduction; the systematization, organization and updating of data. Even the negative response to a request for access entails that the public or private official obliged to invest time, resources and, in certain cases, even economic wear and tear, to meet the request for access to information proposed by a citizen.

In certain cases, it is easy to determine what information is considered public, since it is expressly detailed in the legislative texts. However, legal texts are generally not exhaustive or contain open clauses, or the ambiguity with which they have been drafted makes it impossible to know the true scope of the rule, i.e., to know what to do before a given document or piece of data that bears some element that constitutes public information and another that doesn't. Moreover, the dynamism of social relations precludes a rigid rule that discerns which information will *always* be public and which will *always* be private and confidential. Therefore, an open definition that allows relevant data to be considered public in the future, together with the principle of maximum disclosure and the public interest test, is considered aligned with adequate governmental protection of people's right to information. Gómez Gallardo (2009, 17) coins a term that can guide the application of the legal protection of the right of access to information, in cases of difficult determination: *the right to know*. In a democratic and pluralistic state, openness and government transparency are not options: they are the core of the political structure and administration of public affairs –or should be. In this sense, following the democratic principle pointed out at the beginning of this study, in confusing cases it will be necessary to ask: *What does the citizen need to know?* The answer is *everything that the state does on behalf of the citizen and to his or her personal or collective benefit or detriment*. If the information requested fits this answer, we should be dealing with public information. Consider, for example, the purchase of military equipment. Does the Ministry of Defense make that purchase for a public purpose? Certainly, the defense of national borders is one of the government's duties, therefore, information about the equipment purchased, its price, quality, quantity, etc. is considered public. Therefore, there is a general right to access such information. However, allowing the free flow of tactical military information may jeopardize the country's defense strategy. Consequently, at the same time that the rule guarantees an adequate administration of resources, the state must protect other interests of high importance that may even entail risk for the population. This protection is achieved through legal locks that must pursue a legitimate purpose, in accordance with international treaties on civil and political rights. Laws and public policy must be designed in strict compliance with the permitted restrictions. In this sense, domestic laws (i) define the concept of *public information* and (ii) establish the regime of exemptions to be legally applied to requests for access and/or active dissemination of information.

The object protected by the right of access to public information is, undoubtedly, the information held by state entities, which is produced with public resources. But not all information of public relevance is held by public entities. In certain legal systems (such as the Ecuadorian or Mexican) even information held by private entities (when they provide public services or act in some form of representation of the state) is considered public and is subject to disclosure.

> International relations, corporate control and oversight, social responsibility, the administration of justice, the economy and growth, among other areas, have been affected by this trend towards greater transparency and accountability. As Florini (1998) states, it has even forced countries to cede an important part of their sovereignty, for example, in the area of nuclear arms control. (Del Solar 2008, 94-95).

Accordingly, several Middle Eastern countries, such as Azerbaijan and Kyrgyzstan, also bind private entities through their access to public information laws. The same is true of India (with respect to NGOs) and South Africa. In Europe, the regulations of Bulgaria (obliging entities that use mixed budgets and means) and the United Kingdom (the regulator has the power to include a private entity as public when it exercises public functions) have similar effects on private entities linked to public information (Mendel, 2008). Mexico includes private companies that execute public expenditure and/or exercise authority functions (Villanueva, 2003). As for the Inter-American region, the Peruvian access law is quite similar to the Ecuadorian law, including as obligated subjects all those private entities that provide public services or perform public functions.

The concept of public information differs from one legislation to another, expanding or restricting the protection of its access according to the political theory to which legislators and public policy makers adhere. The above considering, noticeably, that the law is an expression of a country's culture, history and social structure. The nuances are as varied as there are countries in the world that have enacted laws to build institutionality around this right, as required by the international conventions they have ratified or acceded to. Asian legal systems, in terms of access to information, have developed their regulations around the concept of the *right to know*. Thus, for example, as Mendel (2003, 63-64) comments, the Japanese Supreme Court developed *the right to know* around 1969. The South Korean Constitutional Court recognized a similar right between 1989 and 1991. India also links freedom of expression to *the right to know*.

To elaborate on some Western countries, these are the definitions provided in the access to information laws of Argentina, Ecuador, Mexico and the United Kingdom (in alphabetical order):

	Legal body	**Most recent update**	**Definition of "Public Information"**
Argentina	Law No. 27275 Right of Access to Public Information	2016	Any type of data contained in documents of any format generated, obtained, transformed, controlled or kept by the regulated entities.
Ecuador	Organic Law of Transparency and Access to Public Information.	2023	Any kind of data contained in documents of any format, definitive or preparatory, generated or not by the obligated subject, which are in the possession of the subjects bound by this law, contained, created or obtained by them, which are under their responsibility and custody or which have been produced with State resources.
Mexico	Federal Law of Transparency and Access to Public Information.	2021	All information generated, obtained, acquired, transformed or in possession of obligated subjects at the federal level, referred to in the General Law of Transparency and Access to Public Information and the present Law, is public, accessible to any person and may only be qualified exceptionally as temporarily reserved for reasons of public interest and national security or as confidential.
United Kingdom	Freedom of Information Act 2000	2023	For the purposes of this Act, information is held by a public authority if- (a) it is held by the authority, otherwise than on behalf of another person, or (b) it is held by another person on behalf of the authority.

Authorized and Responsible Parties

According to the general theory of law, a subject of law is an individual who possesses the necessary qualities to be considered as an active entity by the legal system, which allows it to exercise rights and fulfill duties. In other words, an entity (whether a physical person, a legal person or others) entitled to act at the legal level, either in its own name or through a representative, is considered an active subject (holder of a right) or a passive subject (enduring the correlative responsibilities of such right). In these two categories, the active legal subject is the one who possesses the power to enjoy and exercise a specific right, and the passive legal subject is the one who is responsible or obliged to perform, carry out or refrain from performing certain actions in accordance with the powers of the active subject. This creates a synallagmatic or bilateral relationship. Perfect bilateral relationships imply that both subjects are mutually obligated to each other, resulting in both subjects acting simultaneously as active and passive entities, albeit under different functions or duties.

Another type of association is the synallagmatic-imperfect connection, when one of the parties possesses a right while the other is only obligated to the first, without receiving direct compensation in return. This is a relationship of subordination. In the framework of human rights theory, the state-citizen relationship can be categorized as subordinate[11]. Thus, in the current democratic model, power lies with the citizens and they elect authorities to represent them, administer public affairs and make decisions. Like any mandatary or agent, those elected authorities and appointed officers are subject to accountability for the acts they perform on behalf of their principal. This principal-agent relationship, in the democratic context, i.e., of *the public*, is well explained by John Ackerman:

> (...) accountability only exists as part of a 'principal-agent relationship', in which the principal delegates authority to his agent, who acts for him, and then holds him accountable for his prior performance (...) Here we see that accountability is a dynamic process that redefines the relationship between state and society, thus reconfiguring the very nature of democracy and citizen participation. (Ackerman 2008, 17-18).

---

[11] As Solimano (2008, 69) further explains, this inversion of subordination is explained in the theory of welfare economics: "The theory of economic policy based on welfare economics assumes that public officials are 'agents' of a 'principal' which is the state, whose highest political authorities respond to a citizen mandate and whose decisions seek, according to this theory, the maximization of social welfare."

In this power scheme, the administered citizens have the *moral responsibility* to defend all the rights that derive from human dignity, while the state has the *legal obligation* to respect, protect, guarantee and promote those rights. Citizens have certain responsibilities and obligations towards the state as part of the social contract, but they are not on the same hierarchical legal level. To simplify the concept, citizens are only obliged to respect the human rights of others, comply with the law and pay taxes. Any other social or political duty is more or less optional (notwithstanding the consequences of unlawful behavior). However, these obligations are neither absolute nor reciprocal. A person who breaks the law is still entitled to his or her human rights, in general terms. Even if such person is sentenced to imprisonment, that is, when they are legally deprived of the right to free movement, their human dignity must still be protected by the state. Therefore, the obligations of citizens are of lesser legal force than the obligations that the state has towards its inhabitants. Every human being, regardless of any distinction or privilege, is an active subject of all human rights[12]. Restrictions are permissible only if they affect the rights of others who have an equivalent level of importance. In short, the core of every human right is human dignity.

Regarding the right of access to public information, private legal entities, as part of the extensive group of governed people within the state structure and subject to its established legal system, can also be considered as entitled subjects. Therefore, a company, a non-governmental organization or a private association all hold the right to be informed just like individual physical persons do. This means that those entities have the right to request information from the state, and this right cannot be rejected on the grounds that they are not human individuals and, therefore, do not have inherent human dignity. For example, Article 42 of the Charter of Fundamental Rights of the European Union guarantees the right of access to "*any natural or legal person residing or having its registered office in a Member State*", thus ratifying the protection of non-human entities. Furthermore, this wording clearly includes persons of another national origin, provided that they are resident in the European Union, reaffirming the universal nature of this right.

Delving into this, we see that freedom of information and expression has historically been recognized to companies working in communications and media, as they are a necessity of a democratic society. Therefore, the state will always act as a passive subject, even if the right holder is not human.

---

[12] In some countries, nature and its elements have been recognized with rights emanating from their dignity and need for survival, either through the law (such as the National Constitution of Ecuador) or through jurisprudence (such as Colombia).

The state does not possess inherent rights, but just the necessary powers and functions that are used to achieve its ultimate goal: the common welfare. These definitions seek certain constantly evolving distinctions in response to social dynamics, making static delimitations insufficient, but maintaining an essence towards achieving the highest possible level of enjoyment of fundamental rights.

The above commentary is relevant in the theoretical and legal realm. In real life, however, the state accumulates an enormous amount of power, which also makes it prone to abuse of individuals. In this factual context, the state is the strong party, so citizens rely on the constitutional framework to protect their dignity and freedom. The primary function of fundamental rights, in representative democracies, is to direct the exercise of power to prevent arbitrariness. Historically, only state officials were obliged to defend the human rights of their population. The neoliberal model has restricted the political and social functions of states, resulting in a state structure that refrains from intervening and instead gives the private sector greater freedom to operate. Depending on the political model, this varies from country to country. However, in a democratic system, human rights abuses have occurred not only by acts of public officials, but also by private individuals who have acquired different types of *de facto authority* over the average citizen. Today, entities such as companies, multinational corporations, foreign states, and other geopolitical and economic actors are increasingly expanding the range of human rights accountability due to their increasing level of economic and political influence. While human rights theory asserts that it is primarily the responsibility of the state to promote, guarantee and protect human rights, due to the accumulation of power and control, various non-state entities now play a secondary role in relation to human rights and may be held accountable for violations to them. This is evident in the right of access to public information, which requires private entities to provide data that the law defines as public or of public interest, such as details on large-scale projects, extractive industries, mass consumer goods or health-related matters.

The issue of access to public information is an intricate one. When it comes to fundamental rights, it is usually clear who is the passive subject. Even when individuals violate these rights, the state is responsible because it is obliged to guarantee the peaceful coexistence and quality of life of its citizens. In other words, the state can become a violator of rights by inaction or omission. Essentially, human rights can be violated both by the state (due to its actions or lack thereof), and by individuals, who have the duty to respect the rights of others. Therefore, the right of access to public information applies not only to the government and the various public entities, but also to individuals who possess information that meets the criteria to be considered public. Cox Irarrázabal, quoted by Rojo A. (2010, 15), highlights the importance of relevant data held by private entities for society, in this imaginary dialogue between society and corporations:

> In an ever-changing world, society's expectations of corporate transparency have also evolved. Trust is decreasing and more and better information about what they are doing is required. In the past people didn't ask for much and companies acted from the notion of *trust me*, I *know how to do things right*. But as people's trust declined, we came to the *word-of-mouth* world, where people start asking for more. Still, trust continued to decline and people began to demand demonstrable information. We entered the *show-me* world, where the company had to prove that what it said it did, it did, and it did it that way and not another way. But the change continues, trust continues to fall and today we are entering the '*certify me*' world.

There is an evident difference between the right to have public information available with other political and civil rights due to the relationship between information and power. Since the very configuration of this right, it has become more and more evident that not only government institutions possess information of general importance, but also private companies or other important actors in the field of information and communication hold socially valuable data. In Ecuador, the Constitution defines the public sector as the group of agencies and companies constituted for the provision of public services and the performance of economic activities that are the responsibility of the state[13], which is complemented by the provisions of the transparency law that make private companies in charge of these public activities responsible for providing public information[14]. In addition, it recognizes the right to obtain accurate and sufficient information on all categories of public services provided within the country's borders. In such cases, individuals are obliged only regarding the information that is considered public. This means that the obligation applies to material that has been developed with public funds or that relates to public services or projects and, ultimately, where a general interest can be demonstrated. In such cases, the acquisition of specific information by any individual is justified, even if it is owned or generated by private bodies.

As for domestic regulations, the Mexican transparency law[15], states that, in addition to state entities, any individual or legal entity or guild that provides and executes public resources, or performs acts of authority, is

[13] Ecuador. Constituent Assembly 2008, Article 215.

[14] Ecuador. National Assembly 2023, Article 8.

[15] Mexico. Cámara de Diputados del H. Congreso de la Nación 2016, Articles 1, 9.

bound by it. Like the Ecuadorian law, the Argentine transparency law has a more detailed list of obligated subjects, which not only includes all companies with state participation, but also concessionaires that provide public services, state contractors in any form, companies, political parties, unions, universities and any private entity that has been provided with public funds, regarding everything related to those, as well as individuals in everything related to public law[16]. As per the United Kingdom Information Act[17], it provides that a person exercising functions of a public nature or providing a service under a contract entered into with a public authority is also bound under it. Thus, when it comes to private individuals, the legal rules provide for their adherence to its rules, but only with respect to information that is deemed *public according* to the law, which means that the principle of transparency here has certain limitations that are not opposable when it comes to essentially public institutions.

To better illustrate this, consider the scenario of a mobile telecommunications service provider: connectivity information, being a public service (under certain legislations), can be requested by any inhabitant of the country. However, interconnection network plans, which may be safeguarded by industrial secrecy, could not be required under transparency laws.

It is important to note that, in general, the law prohibits state authorities from inquiring about the purpose or destination of the information requested by the right holder: the information belongs to the people, whose public authorities are its mere trustees. This is reinforced by the fact that the right of access to information was originated as a component of freedom of expression and, therefore, subject to the same rules of exercise. That is to say that, although freedom of expression is not an absolute right and admits limitations, it is also true that it shall be exercised without prior censorship, but subject to the subsequent imposition of liabilities[18]. This is seen in the Ecuadorian standard discussed above, where no public authority may inquire about the purpose of the information subject to a citizen request. Colombian jurisprudence has also ruled in similar terms:

> Freedom of information has a dual meaning: it refers, on the one hand, to the subjective right of a person to disseminate information without being subjected to disproportionate external coercion and, on the other, to the primary right of the recipient to receive truthful, timely and impartial information. This reaffirms the social responsibility assigned to those who make use of this right.

[16] Argentina. Senate and Chamber of Deputies 2016, Article 7.

[17] UK Parliament 2022, Section 5.

[18] Claude Reyes et al. v. Chile 2006, para. 61.

The ECrtHR also aligns itself with the observance of the general limitations on freedom of expression imposed on the right of access to information by stating that:

> In the Court's view, obtaining access to information would be considered necessary if the refusal would hinder or impair the individual's exercise of his or her right to freedom of expression (see *Társaság,* § 28), including the freedom to "receive and impart information and ideas", in a manner consistent with the "duties and responsibilities" that may arise under Article 10(2)[19].

The prohibition of prior censorship is a long-standing condition for the exercise of freedom of expression. Article 13.2 of the American Convention on Human Rights explicitly states that the rights enshrined in Article 13.1, which includes the right to *seek* information, may not be subject to prior censorship, allowing this type of scrutiny only in public performances, in order to safeguard the rights of children and adolescents. Consequently, countries bound by this instrument may not require a petitioner to disclose his or her intent or purpose for seeking public information. This rule is commonly disregarded by public officials who consistently respond to a request for access with a questioning about the purpose of the search. In human rights investigations, revealing the purpose may impede its achievement. In accordance with this premise, several legal systems prohibit the denial of information in cases of human rights violations, even if it is classified or reserved data. A similar provision is not available in the International Covenant on Civil and Political Rights or in the European Convention. In fact, several ECrtHR rulings seem to lean towards an adequate showing, by the petitioner, that the information is sought for a purpose compatible with the public interest in a democratic society, placing a burden of proof on the petitioner.

Now, in order to shape a definition of *public information*, one must first eliminate any element that does not belong to or exceeds its conceptual boundaries and thus create a precise delimitation that more accurately reflects its meaning. For the purposes of this study, the exemption regime can be divided into two broad sections based on the purpose of protection. These sections are the *private interest exemptions* and *public policy exemptions.*[20]

Personal and confidential data, classified information and other categories fall outside the scope of this fundamental right and cannot be accessed

[19] Magyar Helsinki Bizottsag v. Hungary 2016, para. 158.
[20] Lavalle Cobo, 2009.

through the means provided for by it, in general terms. Governments are responsible for the protection of such information under conditions similar to those to which they are subject with respect to the release of public information. This means that they have the burden of respecting, guaranteeing and protecting personal data because they derive from human dignity as well. This has been recognized in international instruments and state constitutions; that is to say, at the highest normative level. Consequently, they will be required to balance conflicting interests and decide on a reasoned basis, taking into account international standards.

Something similar occurs with public interest exceptions. The state must weigh the harm to society that would result from the dissemination of information that compromises the security of the state or the protection of borders. In such cases, restricting access is the correct option to go with. The decision is not a simple one because sensitive information is often also highly valuable in holding those in power to account. Therefore, the regime of exceptions must be carefully considered (more on this in the next chapter).

In conclusion, it can be affirmed that information that is categorized within the exceptions of public order or protection of personal data cannot be considered *public information.* In such cases, this information is legitimately kept out of the access of individuals. Then, how can it be determined, in each case, that we are dealing with public information that can be disseminated, or, on the contrary, that the information has a restricted nature? The *public interest test* has been developed for this purpose.

Public Interest Test

A common concern among public authorities is that, by granting unrestricted access to all information and documentation, the structure of the state as such may be compromised. To address this substantial concern, both international and domestic law provide for specific rules and a regime of exemptions to legitimately allow governments to keep sensitive information safeguarded. International courts have also established parameters that entitle citizens to access information without undermining the states' structure and functions. The ECrtHR has developed and applied the *public information test* to determine whether freedom of expression was violated in cases where states deny access to certain information. The public interest test "*requires public authorities and supervisory bodies to balance the interest in withholding information against the public interest in disclosure*"[21]. This

[21] Magyar Helsinki Bizottsag v. Hungary 2016, para. 64.

weighs out both ends of the same duty, allowing for the proper treatment of information held by public administrators. The test seeks to evidence that (i) the delivery of information to the public concern relevant matters, essential for the public debate[22]; (ii) that it is made in good faith and under standards of investigation or ethical journalism[23]; and, (iii) that the motivation for such search for information is consistent with those informative purposes. As Upegui (2020, 61) explains:

> The test has two elements: establishing that the disclosure of the personal information satisfies a public interest and demonstrating that the benefits linked to the satisfaction of that interest, via disclosure of the information, justify the sacrifice of the individual's interest in maintaining confidentiality.

The foregoing could suggest a prior analysis of the purposes pursued by the petitioner that would lead to prior censorship. In addition, several of the rulings that have reasoned on the subject consider the search for information in the context of journalism exclusively, ignoring other transcendental uses of information, such as the defense of other fundamental rights, for instance health, the environment and a fair trial, to name those that are part of this study. In cases where the particular interests of a person, a family, a community and even legal persons collide with those of the state, state-owned enterprises or public institutions, proof of public interest information may become a real impediment to access that could lead to prevent the petitioner from the adequate and timely defense of other rights and legitimate interests. It may also degrade public debate on important issues. This test can become quite subjective and puts public officials in a position of *judge and jury*.

Personal interests and the use of information held by public offices are covered by the guarantees of this right in the American circuit, which broadens the spectrum of protection through the definition of public information and its ownership by citizens. UNESCO recognizes the importance of the progress achieved by the jurisprudential line of the ECrtHR, although it still presents obstacles that, in contrast, have been removed by the IACHR.

> The ECtHR has progressively interpreted the right of access to public information as part of the provisions included in Article 10 of the ECHR. However, it should be noted that this protection is still incomplete, partly due to interpretation problems arising from the specific wording of this article. Unlike Article 19 of the International Covenant on Civil and Political

---

[22] Társaság a Szabadságjogokért (TASZ) v. Hungary 2005.

[23] Goodwin v. United Kingdom, 1996.

> Rights or Article 13 of the American Convention, Article 10 mentions the right to "receive and disseminate" information, but omits the verb "to seek" UNESCO (2021, 81).

UNESCO's observation becomes evident when reviewing Gaskin v. United Kingdom (1989, paras. 51-53), in which the ECrtHR emphasized that:

> The Commission found that Article 10 (art. 10) did not, in the circumstances of the case, give the applicant a right to obtain, against thewill of the local authority, access to the file held by that authority. The Government agreed.
>
> The Court holds, as it did in its aforementioned Leander judgment, that "the right to freedom to receive information basically prohibits a Government from restricting a person from receiving information that others wish or may be willing to impart to him." (Series A no. 116, p. 29, para. 74). Also in the circumstances of the present case, Article 10 (art. 10) does not embody an obligation on the State concerned to impart the information in question to the individual.
>
> There has thus been no interference with Mr Gaskin's right to receive information as protected by Article 10 (art. 10).

In Norman v. United Kingdom (2021) the European judges went as far as assessing the intimate and personal motivations of the information provider. This case dealt with a former prison officer (the plaintiff) convicted for providing information to the media on certain internal aspects that he could only know about because he was employed there. The information had been given to a newspaper in exchange for money. The ECrtHR dismissed the charge of violation of Article 10 of the European Convention on Human Rights, alleged by the prison officer after he had been sanctioned for this behavior. The practical question this case leaves us with is: can you write straight with crooked lines? The Court considered two important issues:

(i) There was no public interest in most of the information disclosed by the applicant, and he was not motivated by public interest concerns in doing so, as his personal dislike for the prison director and the payment received by the recipient of such information were the real triggers, as determined by the country's courts.

(ii) The public interest in prosecuting the plaintiff to maintain the integrity and effectiveness of the prison service and the public's confidence in it outweighed the claimant's personal interest in secretly disseminating privileged information to which he had access, in the context of his work as a prison officer.

This is a rather interesting case, as the facts, at first glance, suggested that the public's interest in the management of the prison system and of a specific unit would outweigh the damage to the reputation of its managers, who are public officials, and of the system itself, provided that the information was accurate and properly substantiated. However, on closer analysis of the information *sold* by the applicant, the domestic courts concluded otherwise, and the ECrtHR upheld the correct application of the sentence by dismissing the case. It would be accurate to say that this case's outcome could have been different had it been heard in the Inter-American circuit. Since the purpose sought by the petitioner in requesting access is not a relevant factor for the Inter-American system, it cannot become a ground for sanctioning the disclosing officer (even if the internal work rules were not observed) given that the importance of the right of access outweighs the disciplinary statutes. Consistent with the above, neither can it become an obstacle to the delivery of the requested information. The purpose of acquiring the information, on the other hand, is to disseminate it for public deliberation. Therefore, such a purpose cannot be predetermined by the state, at the risk of incurring prior censorship. Moreover, since it is a fundamental right that implies, *prima facie*, duties of abstention for the state, and the guarantee of the widest possible exercise for the holder of the right, a prior inquiry into the subjective motives of the applicant for information seems incompatible with the notion of a *fundamental right*. Furthermore, as this is a fundamental entitlement that entails the state's duty to abstain from interference and ensure the broadest possible exercise of the right, conducting a preliminary investigation into the personal motivations of the individual seeking information is inconsistent with the essence of this fundamental right. In the chapters to come, it will be demonstrated that governments should refrain from intervening in the private exercise of this right and should strive to achieve its utmost level of enjoyment for every acknowledged right.

However, the Norman v. United Kingdom case highlights what Upegui (2020) calls the "public-private dichotomy". Beyond the collision between the principle of maximum disclosure and the protection of trust in a public system –in this case, the prison system–, the facts described therein show that there is a permanent confrontation between the citizens' interest in accessing and the public interest in safeguarding information. This dichotomy allows one to recognize the need for a case-by-case approach, so long as both interests are protected by the constitution and the law.

Based on this premise, even when it is stated that the petitioner cannot be required to expose, in advance, his or her motives regarding the information collected or disseminated –a concept clearly developed in the

Inter-American circuit, we insist– its intention and management must be adequate to the fundamental right in every case. It is not disputed that the exercise of this right is subject to limitations, nor that any harm that may be caused to others if the information is improperly managed or disseminated, must be compensated and sanctioned. However, it is asserted that this analysis is highly dangerous and even undemocratic if done *prior to* the release and dissemination of information or, when grounded on subjective, unclear parameters. In Norman v. United Kingdom (2021), the ECrtHR found that the state had not violated the Convention by sanctioning the prison officer (the applicant) who gave information from a public prison to a newspaper *because* his intention had never been to feed public opinion with facts of interest but to discredit a superior officer. Ahead of the comparison between the levels and characteristics of supranational protection, the collision of rights between access to public information and its dissemination vis-à-vis the reputation of others is evident in this case. Conversely, considering such intimate motives is dangerous and subjective. In view of this, the Mexican transparency authorities "*agree that personal information is only of interest to the subject, it is the property of the person, and its knowledge does not obey nor is called to satisfy any public interest*"[24], which would settle a good number of cases in which this collision is present. In similar cases, someone's personal information could be inserted in some way in documents that by law are considered public, but in which it must be *reasoned* whether their free dissemination is appropriate in the face of a catalog of interrelated rights of equal hierarchy.

In light of the above, the public interest test is material to solve doubtful petitions of access that deal with personal or restricted information. A proper public interest test requires objective standards, provided for in the law prior to the filing of the petition, and they should be useful to allow the obliged authority to weigh out the interests at hand and make a proper decision. Such a decision, additionally, must be prone to be revised by an upper or judicial authority to guarantee that it meets human rights standards.

Reasonableness Test

The concept of reasonableness is the most important factor to take into account when it comes to the limitations imposed on the right of access to information, and to human rights in general. This is because the supremacy of these rights over other interests of a lesser order requires that the adverse effect that the person will endure when his or her human right is reduced in

---

[24] Upegui Mejía 2020, 55.

favor of that of another person be justified within the parameters of the irreducible core of that right. The question of reasonableness has been fruitfully discussed in the development of the theory of equality and prohibition of discrimination. In analyzing the way in which the IACrtHR handles discrimination cases, Dulitzky (2007) delivers the *reasonableness test* that is within the view of the judges in charge of ruling on such cases. As occurs in the general human rights regime, limitations to access to public information may be the product of discrimination when it obeys, not to objective criteria, but to certain conditions of the person. For example, when information is restricted to a union member or a community leader. A restriction imposed on the exercise of a given right to a person, under a category suspected of discrimination, will be considered lawful only if it is shown that such a measure is necessary for the protection of another right of the same hierarchy and that there are no other means to avoid such restriction or impairment. This test is valid for restrictions related to access to public information.

> Generally, this test requires that the purpose of the measure be legitimate and important, but also imperative. The means chosen must not only be appropriate and indeed conducive, but also necessary, i.e., it cannot be replaced by an alternative means that is less harmful. In addition, the assessment of proportionality requires that the benefits of adopting the measure clearly outweigh the restrictions imposed on other principles and values. (Dulitzky, 2007, 20).

From this author's perspective, the reasonableness test can be divided into three components: (i) the end or purpose of the measure; (ii) the means selected to achieve that end; and, (iii) the greater benefit achieved through the restriction, as compared to the hypothetical outcome of the other available options. Therefore, reasonableness leads to the next level of enforceability with respect to state activities: it is the authority's responsibility to demonstrate that its activity is properly constructed in accordance with constitutional precepts. This means that the burden of proof lies on the public authority.

In addition, democracy requires a significant degree of transparency, with limitations deemed legitimate only if and when they are consistent with the principles of a democratic society. As indicated above, the default principle is that information *is* public, with secrecy being the exception. In such circumstances, the burden of proof is on public administrators to demonstrate the need to restrict certain information or data from the public, just as they must demonstrate the need for the restrictions to conform to the legal standards in force. Generally speaking, a request for access may only be denied if a competent authority has classified the information as secret, confidential or reserved (in accordance with domestic law) *prior* to the submission of the request, or if such information relates to the privacy or confidential data of private persons (such as medical records, industrial or professional secrecy, political affiliations, criminal records or other protected information). Otherwise, the information is considered public, so anyone interested in it has the right to *know it*. Denying it, then, will be considered illegal and in most states, unconstitutional.

While in some legislations this approach is quite broad, in other states the level of secrecy is much higher. In some cases, the warmongering history of certain states produces a tendency toward secrecy and hermeticism in the public sphere. In other instances, opacity serves unutterable interests because it produces an environment conducive to corruption or segregation. In fact, experts that have studied the phenomenon of corruption find a need for regulation and transparency in various activities that often operate in ethical gray areas:

> (...) regulation of political financing, government procurement systems, regulation of lobbying, transparency and publicity of legislative processes, systems for regulating conflicts of interest such as declarations of assets and interests, among others. All of them tend to make decisions and their processes more observable, besides improving control capacity, which together favors greater probity and generates a higher respect for the public interest over private interests (...) Access to public information as a general tool complements and reinforces specific regulations and expands their logic to other areas where they do not exist. (Del Solar 2008, 97-98, 101)

Another circumstance adverse to transparency is the protection of public officials –and other actors, even in private enterprises and NGOs– of their own jobs. When information is disseminated, the focus falls more deeply on resource management and decision making. Thus, as they are exposed to greater scrutiny, they are also exposed to greater risk of removal from the position that is the source of their livelihood and, in the worst case, of unjustified wealth:

> (...) to the extent that the ease of access to public information is extended, the scope of corruption, influence peddling, the incidence of money in politics and clientelism is restricted and efficiency is improved.
>
> Despite the benefits associated with a more transparent public administration, from the point of view of the agencies generating information, be they companies or NGOs, the incentives to maintain secrecy are greater.

> (...) every decision-maker faces the possibility of errors or omissions coma. For this reason, they tend to prefer secret procedures limited to a minimum number of participants, since comma when it comes to relevant decisions, there is also the risk of leaks. (Del Solar 2008, 101-102).

Whatever the case may be, openness is an international mandate and if the state has ratified treaties that protect access to information, it is obliged to orient its apparatus to achieve that end. International standards hold that any restriction or limitation must be established by law (and not by second-order regulations or policies or individual decisions of the authorities) and must be justified as necessary to protect other fundamental rights such as public health, national security or public order.

The UK Freedom of Information Act 2000 (as amended from time to time) sets two conditions for excluding information from the public domain:

(i) Absolute exemption provided by the same law, in Part II[25] (an objective criterion).
(ii) When the public interest in maintaining the exemption prevails over the public interest in disclosing the information (a subjective criterion, which requires proof to support the decision to disclose or not, on the grounds of the reasonableness test).

It is noteworthy that many constitutions make specific provisions for openness in cases of gross human rights violations. In such cases, any barrier to access is eliminated, even if the legal standards for keeping information locked up are met. These norms imply a step forward from the Inter-American standard: in these legislations there is not only maximum publicity but also an absolute prohibition of withholding information. It underscores the overriding need to safeguard human rights above all other considerations. If a request for access to public information is filed because the required piece of information or document is necessary to denounce or investigate a case of human rights violation, there are no barriers, whether public or private. This is the text of this Ecuadorian constitutional norm, as an example:

> Article 18. Every person, individually or collectively, has the right to: (...)
> 2. Free access to information generated by public or private entities that manage State funds or perform public functions. There shall be no

[25] Among others: information accessible to the public by other means; information intended for future publication; judicial records, parliamentary privilege; personal information, information provided on a confidential basis, professional secrecy, etc.

> reservation of information except in cases expressly stipulated by law. In case of violation of human rights, no public entity shall deny information.

Now, to resolve ambiguous cases in which the *right to know* and other constitutional protections clash, guiding principles have been developed. There is no perfect recipe. In each case, the interests at stake must be balanced and the one that is of lesser value (as per the facts of the case under examination) must render before the one that prevails. This implies an intellectual exercise, if not of sensitivity, of the conditions and characteristics of the case.

Principles

Legal institutions are distinguished by their foundational principles, which serve as a compass to indicate the direction in which legal provisions point. A legal principle refers to a widely recognized rule that facilitates the understanding and application of a norm, thus providing clarity in situations where there is ambiguity, absence of a specific rule, or inconsistencies. Legal principles are considered a mandate to achieve the highest possible level of protection of a fundamental right.

The philosophy of transparency and the right to information may have different foundations in different regions, but the principles are generally universal and have been established by legal precedents, theoretical frameworks and social developments, among other significant historical events. The principles can be identified within the framework of local law, although it is often necessary to examine the supranational context to bring clarity to the domestic framework. To have a deeper understanding of their origin, it is key to gather the cases and social contexts that were associated with them. The following principles are of cardinal importance in the field of information rights theory.

Maximum Disclosure

The principle of maximum disclosure is widely considered to be the main guiding principle in relation to the protection of freedom of expression and its associated guarantees, including public transparency. This concept postulates that any information held by the government is rendered public. Accordingly, the rule dictates that the government is obliged to provide access to such information to its citizens. Only in extraordinary circumstances, as provided by law, may such material be held in confidence. This principle gives rise to such features as genuine accessibility, promptness of disclosure, and the manner in which requests for information must be dealt with, even in cases where the information is partially confidential. The fundamental principle of freedom of access to information centers on the idea of maximum disclosure.

Claude Reyes v. Chile (2006) set a significant legal precedent for the Americas in terms of access to justice, burden of proof in case of denial of access, relevance of information for the public, and partially disclosable information. It mandated that states must comply with a minimum of three obligations to justify any restriction on access to public information:

(i) Compatibility of such limitations with Inter-American standards on freedom of expression.
(ii) Evidence that the dissemination of information threatens to cause substantial harm to a legitimate purpose under the Convention.
(iii) That the potential harm outweighs the public's interest in having the information available.

In short, when faced with a situation in which a human right guaranteed by the Constitution or international instruments conflicts with the right of access, it becomes necessary to make an assessment to determine which right should prevail, as well as the extent to which the other right may be compromised. The state is obliged to restrict the ability to access information only through a rational process, which must be explicit and reasoned before the petitioner and the people. This precedent also clarified that the petitioner cannot be compelled to state the reason for such a request, since if the information is the property of the people, access to it is mandatory.

Derived from the principle of maximum disclosure, the IACrtHR developed the *proportionality* test applicable to the right of access:

> According to the general terms of Article 13, the right of access to information must be governed by the "principle of maximum disclosure". The burden of proof falls on the State, which must demonstrate that the limitations on access to information are compatible with Inter-American standards on freedom of expression. (...)
>
> This means that the restriction must not only refer to one of the objectives, but it must also be shown that the disclosure constitutes a threat of substantial harm to that objective and that the harm to the objective must outweigh the public interest in having the information (Claude Reyes v. Chile 2006, 36).

To resolve the requirements for information that is partially public and partially confidential, the Inter-American Transparency Law Model (OAS, 2020) provides the following rule, ensuring the highest possible level of transparency and openness:

> In those circumstances in which the entirety of the Information contained in a Document is not exempt from disclosure in accordance with the exceptions (…), a version of the document must be generated that blacks out or covers only the portions of the Document subject to the exception. The non-exempt Information shall be made public and delivered to the applicant.

This seemingly easy effort to ensure accessibility in all cases involving public information has become part of the standards to which states are bound, particularly because state officials tend to deny access in such cases, rather than deciding in favor of the right. If a law provides for such cases, refusals by public bodies will be considered unfounded and illegitimate. Several laws on access to information maintain similar provisions; for example, the Hungarian "Law on the Protection of Personal Data and Disclosure of Information of Public Interest" of 1992, documented by the ECrtHR in Magyar Helsinki Bizottsag v. Hungary (2016, para. 32), resolves this issue by the following solution:

> If a document containing information of public interest also contains data that cannot be disclosed to the applicant, this data must be deleted or unrecognizable in the copy[26] .

In the environmental context, the Escazú Agreement introduced the principle of maximum disclosure at the conventional level, gaining great relevance. Considering that Claude Reyes v. Chile dates from 2006 and that the Agreement was adopted in 2018, one can appreciate the evolution of this right and the importance for the Americas, recognized by the signatory states. In order to guarantee access to environmental information and participation in decisions that may affect its elements, it recognizes a series of basic human rights principles, applied to the purposes of the Agreement. Among them, the principle of maximum disclosure is enshrined in Article 3(h). In addition, the Escazú Agreement also introduced the *public interest test* along with the obligation to weigh conflicting interests when a request is made or when disclosure of environmental data is mandatory (Article 5(9)):

[26] Article 20, 4.

> In applying the public interest test, the competent authority shall weigh the interest in keeping the information and the public benefit resulting from making it public, based on elements of appropriateness, necessity and proportionality.

In addition, the principle of favorability applied to access to public information, requires that, in case of doubt, the right of access to the requested data must prevail. The principle of *in dubio pro petitor* (or, in case of doubt, to opt in favor of the petitioner) has been incorporated into Argentina's federal transparency law[27], not only for the federal entities but for any provincial access to information law. The Escazú Agreement contemplates the *pro homine* principle in Article 3(k), which should be interpreted as covering the rights of nature in places where legal personality has been recognized to nature or its elements, since it provides for the elimination of barriers to the enjoyment of rights. Therefore, these general principles of human rights reinforce the particular principle of maximum disclosure of public information.

Good Faith

According to Talya Uçaryılmaz, the principle of good faith has regained relevance in modern law and is present in most legal relations, including in the application of international law. This author explains that:

> The natural law principle of *bona fides* has always had two requirements: The absence of *dolus* (deceit) and the obligation to behave according to *aequitas naturalis* (natural equity). Accordingly, the principle of good faith started to create implied obligations deriving from the laws of nature (...) Such natural ties unite all human beings, states or all actors in a legal relationship equally (Uçaryılmaz 2020, 50).

This principle is embodied in the Vienna Convention on the Law of Treaties (1969), Article 26 of which states: "*Every treaty in force is binding upon the parties to it and must be performed by them in good faith.*" This principle is one of the pillars of public international law; without it, international treaties would have no real legal mandate, taking into account, nonetheless, that not all types of non-compliance can be brought before international courts. In this sense, this principle implies that international treaties that have been duly and legally executed and have entered into force, must be treated in the same way that a law for the parties thereto, since they are a manifestation of sovereignty. Therefore, considering that the right of access

[27] Argentina. Senate and Chamber of Deputies 2016, Article 1.

is broadly enshrined in international conventions, it becomes clear that this principle is applicable and enforceable.

The principle of good faith is a corollary of the dual process of delivery-reception of public information and is expressly recognized as a standard in the Escazú Agreement for environmental data. But this principle is not applicable only in such context, since it is a general principle of law. Good faith will mandate, for example, that the government refrains from generating propaganda of the political party in office, with public resources, under the pretext of *informing*.

Good faith, in simple terms, implies that the state is obliged to deliver information without hidden intentions, acting reasonably and with a view to complying with the primary objective of guaranteeing fundamental rights, even if this entails limiting prerogatives or expanding duties inherent to the administration of public resources. This, of course, cannot interfere with the services that the state must perform, since deliberative processes cannot oppose or suspend the exercise of other rights, which are often strongly related to the state's role as an economic actor.

Good faith is found in Argentina's federal access to information law, which is interpreted as a mandate for the authorities to interpret the law in such a way that it serves its purpose, to guarantee the application of this right, to provide the necessary means to the petitioners and to do so with due diligence, loyalty and professionalism[28].

Now, to see this principle in action, a case study: consider the potential conflict of interest that could arise when information requested by an individual or group is used to initiate legal action against the government. The principle of good faith requires the provision of information in a prompt and proper manner, without any withholding, in a way that balances the interests of the parties involved, thus enabling both parties to fully act and defend themselves in the legal proceedings. In order to achieve equality within the process, the law may require that the burden of proof be assigned to the state or whoever possesses the relevant information[29] to guarantee the right to a fair trial, which is also established as a human right through the European and Inter-American Conventions. This protects the search for truth and justice as the primary objectives of access to justice.

---

[28] Argentina. Senate and Chamber of Deputies 2016, article 1.

[29] As an example, Ecuador's law of constitutional guarantees mandates the reversal of the burden of proof in cases involving environmental or nature rights, discrimination or other types of subordination.

Contestability

Another important principle concerns contestability, which pertains to the concrete ability to challenge an administrative decision that denies access, regardless of whether it is stated explicitly or in an implicit way. This notion is intricately connected to the legal recourse that is available to obtain pertinent information in cases where this right has been infringed upon. As a result, it has evolved as a guiding principle in the legal system, but mostly has been established under the remedies portion of most statutes. Nevertheless, the inability to contest the unfavorable response –or absence thereof– of a government official would lead to the erosion of the right to get public information. Adequate judicial recourse is essential for the preservation of any basic right.

According to Article 25 of the Inter-American Convention on Human Rights[30], everyone is entitled to a simple and effective remedy to safeguard his or her fundamental rights, even in cases where the right has been violated by a government entity or authority. Given that this treaty further guarantees the right of access to information as an integral component of freedom of expression, it is indisputable that a flexible remedy should be granted in cases where access to public information has been denied. In addition to this recognition, the implementation of measures that allow the exercise of the right to access in cases in which it has been violated or in which the citizen cannot do so without the tutelage of the state itself, arises from the duty to guarantee rights that derives from their recognition by the state. In light of the above, a judicial remedy is mandatory in all legislations.

This premise is supported by the IACrtHR, which has repeatedly pointed out that part of the right of access to justice, especially in environmental disputes, is the material possibility of challenging any rule, decision, act or omission of the authorities. The ECtHR has reached the same conclusion[31].

---

[30] Right to judicial protection

Everyone has the right to simple and prompt recourse, or any other effective recourse, to a competent court or tribunal for protection against acts that violate his fundamental rights recognized by the constitution or laws of the state concerned or by this Convention, even though such violation may have been committed by persons acting in the course of their official duties.

2. The States Parties undertake to:

a. Ensure that any person claiming such a remedy has his rights determined by the competent authority provided for by the legal system of the State;

b. to develop the possibilities of judicial recourse; and

c. ensure that the competent authorities enforce such remedies when granted.

[31] Inter-American Convention on Human Rights 2017, paras. 235, 237.

Under certain laws, a complaint may be processed before an administrative entity designated to safeguard rights or ensure transparency, such as the Ombudsman, or before an entity specialized in the protection of transparency and access to public information (which in several states also deals with the protection of personal data). In addition, there are judicial remedies established by law specifically to guarantee access to and proper handling of information in public hands.

This topic will be discussed in more detail in the Enforceability chapter.

Liability

The Ecuadorian Transparency Law contemplates accountability and the primacy of the public interest in its charter of principles. While transparency and its essential elements can be considered as fundamental principles of the right to information itself, and therefore informative principles, it is also true that one of the objectives set forth by nations in recognizing the right of access to information is the need to hold public officials accountable for their actions in the administration of the *public res*. This standard provides a concise but meaningful justification for the right of access to information in the context of accountability and fight against corruption: persons exercising public functions must be accountable to those who, having entrusted them with that authority, are affected by their actions[32]. Thus, the right of access to information enables one of the dimensions of the social being: its participation in public affairs and, at the same time, its duty to bring to account those who represent the people, either by vote or by appointment.

Gratuity

It is not the least important principle but probably the most practical one. Among the most damaging barriers to access to any fundamental social benefit right is the cost. Whether dealing with health, education or justice: the cost to the state of implementing these services is always high if we consider that there is no direct compensation, and the national treasuries must cover the needs of the entire population. The human rights catalogs, supported by the interpretative development of supranational bodies, promote free access to rights. The right to information is not exempt from this structure. Treaties on this right, especially the most recent ones, such as the Escazú Agreement, provide for free access as a principle. So do

[32] Ecuador. National Assembly 2023, Article 5 (k).

domestic laws; examples of this are the transparency laws of Argentina, Ecuador and Mexico, which provide for the free provision of information and allow only the charging of reproduction costs, at market value. The United Kingdom Freedom of Information Act provides that fees may be charged only if they are provided for in a regulation, except in cases where a regulation demands proactive disclosure of the information requested. Indeed, the standard requires that the costs of access should not be so high as to be depriving and thus deter the public from seeking access. In addition, the expected costs (whether for reproduction or management) must be proportional to what the state must invest to comply with the necessary administrative task to deliver the requested information[33]. And this is only logical considering that taxpayers have already paid for the processing, security and maintenance of such information.

The use of technology can streamline the process of requesting and receiving public information, making it more efficient and accessible to all individuals, mitigating the costs of delivery. This can help ensure that the right to access information is upheld and protected in a timely manner. Thanks to them, not only can the cost of paper and ink (and its environmental impact) be practically eliminated, but also the cost of mobilization of the petitioner. However, they can also become a barrier to access for certain population groups, such as the elderly, people with disabilities, and people with little schooling in developing countries or rural areas. In order to comply with the principle of free access, means of access should be provided as broadly as possible, taking into account these particular issues of the population or specific groups, avoiding discriminatory treatment of such groups.

The Inter-American Law Model proposes a rule whereby a person who demonstrates a lack of financial means to access the requested information is assisted by the state to obtain the information free of charge (Article 50.2). Similarly, the Escazú Agreement allows the petitioner to be exempted from paying the costs of reproduction or transmission if the person is under a vulnerability condition. Furthermore, these costs must be established in advance, be informed to the petitioner in the first place and be at market value[34], since the exercise of the right cannot be burdensome for the citizen and discourage access or become a source of profit for the state agent.

---

[33] Del Solar 2008, 130.

[34] Soberón Garreta and Trinidad Alvarado 2023, 182.

Characteristics of Public Information

To ensure the successful distribution of information to the public and enable well-informed decision-making, it is crucial for public information to gather certain characteristics that enhance its credibility and usefulness. These traits are essential for fostering openness and reliability within the public sector. When information is deemed doubtful, its content becomes irrelevant, exacerbating the existing conditions of legal, political, and social uncertainty. The characteristics that public information must bear are delineated in many legal instruments, comprising specific international treaties and domestic legislation. These instruments have defined specific aspects as the necessary standards that all information must adhere to in order to fulfill the right to access information.

Such features have been developed through the advancement of theories revolving around the right to information, but not only that: their importance has been evaluated by supranational courts. To this end, the jurisprudential progress of the Inter-American Court has been prolific. According to its rulings, it is required that public information fulfills certain requirements such as clarity, completeness and accuracy:

> In fulfilling this obligation, States must act in good faith so that their actions guarantee the satisfaction of the general interest and do not undermine the confidence of individuals in the administration of the State. Therefore, they must provide and disseminate clear, complete, timely, accurate and updated information.

Not all data are covered by the right to communicate, and the right of access to public information does not cover all messages. Opinions, such as those expressed on the basis of freedom of expression, the dissemination of news through freedom of the press, the custody of correspondence, private communications, and even rumors, are all considered messages. However, not all of these messages are protected by law and some may even be considered infringements of the right to information. Such is the case with rumors, disinformation and certain propaganda. The primary objective of the information protection system must be to deter the dissemination of messages that *manipulate* public opinion, thus compromising the effectiveness of citizen control of the public affairs and decision-making in both the public and private spheres. At this point, the mechanisms of accountability for freedom of expression are activated. These mechanisms serve a variety of purposes, including the prohibition of spreading of rumors and erroneous, biased or malicious information. Such messages are detrimental to the rights of others and to the public interest. Discriminatory messages or advocacy of hate crimes, terrorism, war, or other types of crimes are also prohibited. Therefore, only truthful, verifiable, objective and socially relevant messages deserve legal protection. According to Uicich (1999, 73):

> Only truthful information is that which can be considered [protected] information (...). The right to information is infringed when information is lied about, biased or erroneously misinforms beyond good faith (...) Any requirement for accuracy of data protects the information and the system itself.

Beyond the description of the core of this right from the tools of legal language, it is necessary to know its content in practice. Information as a whole may be subdivided into its components. Following Uicich (1999, 45-46), these concepts can be outlined as:

- **Data**: is the fundamental unit of knowledge that is stored in different supports before being processed and categorized. It is subclassified into:
- **Anonymous data**: it does not allow to determine the person to whom it corresponds, such as statistical data. Normally, anonymous data is always rendered publicly available.
- **Nominative data**: data that allows, in any form, directly or indirectly, the identification of the persons to whom they apply. Certain restrictions may be applied to protect human rights, such as the prohibition of discrimination or the right to private and family life.
- **Sensitive nominal data**: are data that affect the privacy of a person; commonly, they are related to internationally prohibited discrimination criteria, classified as race or ethnicity, skin color, sex, gender, language, religion, political opinions, national or social origin, economic position, place of birth or other social condition that makes the person vulnerable to unequal treatment. Normally, the law establishes specific rules for the processing, storage and deletion of this type of data. Making it publicly available may hinder the exercise of individual rights.
- **Database**: is the container where data will be recorded and kept, modified, updated or deleted. It includes the tools needed to process or retrieve the data (e.g. computer tools such as an electronic index).
- **Information**: It is *"the set of data that allows to give form and content to the whole environment that surrounds it and that*

> *allows by some means... to be assimilated to another being of its same species and cause effects on it...*"[35]. From a strictly legal perspective, according to the Law on Access to Public Information of the City of Buenos Aires (Argentina), "*information is considered to be any type of written, photographic, recorded, magnetic, digital or any other type of documentation that serves as the basis for an administrative act, as well as the minutes of official meetings*".[36]

According to European Community Regulation 1049/2001, still in use today, any medium containing information is considered to be a *document* accessible through the rules on public information. Article 3 mentions the paper version, electronic storage, sound, visual and audiovisual recordings, without this being understood as an exhaustive listing. This exemplary list is important because it shifts from the generic concept of document to all types of information, which is highly important in a society that more and more operates virtuality. Moreover, audiovisual information is often mentally excluded from the scope of access rules, restricting the population of this type of content by means of access requests.

Truthfulness

As stated above, only truthful information is subject to legal protection, so that the obligated institutions are required to provide reliable information, therefore, previously verified by its administrator. The Colombian Constitutional Court has determined that the passive subjects of the communication process –i.e., the public– must demand that the information be truthful and impartial. For the cited Court these characteristics are "*implicit and essential to the guaranteed right*", and, on the contrary, "[information] *that is provided by exceeding the enunciated limits... performs anti-values (falsehood, partiality) and, therefore, does not enjoy legal protection; on the other hand, it has to be sanctioned and rejected...*"[37]. The notion of values and anti-values provided by this high Court is remarkable and helps to understand the importance of information (improperly) delivered to citizens.

---

[35] Ríos Estavillo 2003, 187.

[36] Abramovich and Courtis 2000. Del Solar (2008) also refers to the fact that the format in which the data is found is not relevant for its treatment as public information, to be delivered to the population.

[37] Decision of the Fifth Chamber of the Constitutional Court of Colombia, cited by Gómez Gallardo, 2011, Module I, 7.

Uicich (1999) also includes in his study the right *not* to receive distorted information. Ríos Estavillo (2003) also considers that:

> It is not enough to receive only the transmission of news or data given... [it is] required that such information has a true content; otherwise the person would be receiving false data that would leave him alienated from reality, and therefore, to the detriment of those who do know it.

In the coinciding opinions of these authors, the inequality caused by the lack of truthfulness in information would be detrimental to the right to information. Ríos Estavillo also elaborates this criterion on a forceful sentence of the Spanish Constitutional Court (2003, 189): "*Truthfulness constitutes the 'internal limit' of freedom of information*".

Public information must be verifiable, which implies the responsibility of those who produce, use and distribute it. For Del Solar (2008, 95) reliability is a *sine qua non* factor of state information because the state organisms are the very source of its production. Verifiability is understood as:

> the possibility of establishing, by any plausible means, that the organization's decisions and processes were carried out in the same way as they were defined by the rules... or in the way they are said to have actually occurred (Carbonell, 2010, 247-248).

Accuracy also requires that the information be up to date. When, on the contrary, it is outdated, the normal use of the data is impeded, and the delivery of the information loses its purpose. Therefore, it is a standard of access to information that it should be adjusted to the current reality. An example of this is Directive 2003/4/EC of the European Parliament, which establishes the obligation to adopt measures to organize and update the environmental information held by the member states of the Union (Pigrau Solé 2008, 95). Carbonell (2007), is also of the opinion that:

> It is necessary for such information to be up to date in order to properly exercise this right [of access to information]. If a citizen has data from several years ago, his right of access to public information cannot be fully exercised.

But at this point, it is necessary to define what veracity is. Zaffore, quoted by Lavalle Cobo (2009, 23), states that "*truthfulness in information should be understood as the acceptable correspondence between what has happened and what has been transmitted*". The information, according to the author, must be accurate, reliable and verifiable. When such characteristics are not met, it will not be useful for the purpose for which the citizen requests it, and therefore, agreeing with the previous authors, it cannot enjoy legal protection. In addition, false information may lead to wrong decisions that could well affect other vital legal assets, such as life and freedom. Take, for instance, an arbitrary detention: if the information of the place of imprisonment is misleading, the perpetrators will not be intercepted promptly. Consequently, the provision of such lack of information cannot be considered as compliant with the international and legal obligations incumbent upon the state.

Quality

The application of standards under which information is collected and systematized leads to guaranteeing high quality information. The poorer the standard, the greater the level of arbitrariness that a public official will incur. If data is not treated under certain quality rules, it will not be reliable, relevant and timely available. In order to guarantee the quality of the information, it is essential that it retains its properties intact, carefully ensuring that its essence is not distorted through its handling, not only when it is stored (whether by physical or electronic means), but also when it is processed, including the procedures of systematization, conservation, publication, dissemination and delivery to the petitioner. Ávila Santamaría (2007, 33) states that, since the information belongs to the citizenry, it is incumbent on public bodies to take the utmost care in its administration, since it is a general legal rule that "*the administrator must take extreme care when having in his possession what belongs to another person*". The author explains that "*from a negative perspective, people will be violating the law when they hide, alter or lose information*".

According to Pigrau Solé (2008), the European Parliament includes quality as a parameter that public environmental information must meet in order to guarantee the right of access to it: *"Public authorities must ensure that environmental information is understandable, accurate and comparable, and are also obliged to disclose the collection procedures..."*. Therefore, quality is obtained as a result of compliance with legal, but also technical requirements which include proper systematization programs.

Integrity

Several secondary legislative bodies provide for the adequacy of the information to be delivered to the citizens. In accordance with this premise, in Ecuador the right to adequate and truthful information in the commercial context has been elevated to constitutional rank (Article 66.25). Likewise, Ecuador's Organic Law on Consumer Protection stipulates the obligation of suppliers of goods or services to provide complete information on what they offer, including the risks that such goods and services may entail. This rule is similar in environmental law, where the state is required to provide sufficient information on the risks and adverse impacts that a given activity or project will potentially generate, and not only to disseminate its positive characteristics[38]. Since the Constitution of Ecuador includes consumers and users as a vulnerable group, the protection of their rights has constitutional rank.

Notwithstanding the foregoing, there are cases in which it is permitted to mutilate documents and thus deliver them incomplete to the requester. This is recommended when there are sections in a public document protected by the regime of exceptions (to be discussed in the Exceptions Regime chapter) that cannot be published because to do so would violate legitimate rights such as privacy, trade secret, national security or other protected interests. In order to apply the principle of maximum disclosure, it is essential to provide all information that is considered public *and* deliverable from a given source. That which is to be held in reserve must be blacked out or removed from the version to be provided to the requester to meet both standards.

Adequacy

Adequacy means to accommodate or appropriate something for a purpose, i.e., to assemble the data in a given context. This obligation is not general, but specific to certain types of information, such as those related to the environment or health. The objective of this right to information is to provide real data to citizens for proper decision making. However, according to the nature of the information, it may have more specific purposes. For example, the data collected by the Ministry of Health will be oriented to the production of information related to public health in its multiple aspects, so that it is adequate for these purposes, and therefore, the state will be obliged to provide data with that orientation. Data found in the Ministry of Health that is not useful for understanding health services cannot be considered adequate, and its holding could even be violating individual rights if they fall into any of the suspect categories of discrimination. For example, the Ministry of Health may and should make public information on the supplying of antiretroviral drugs for AIDS

[38] See, for example, Article 2(c) of the Escazú Agreement.

treatment; however, it may not make public the list of patients that have received those, as that information is not adequate for the complete understanding of health services, and instead may produce stigma and discrimination against those beneficiaries (cfr. Personal Data chapter).

On the other hand, extensive, broad or superficial data may be inadequate if it is not systematized with a clear objective in view. Argentine justice has determined that information is inadequate when it is generalized, as stated in the Moreno et al. v. Buenos Aires ruling (Lavalle Cobo, 2009). This means that depositing relevant information in a sea of data does not meet transparency standards and may even become a form of concealment.

Comprehensibility

Public information, being considered the property of citizens, must be accessible to them in terms of comprehension, which means that it must be written in an understandable language –not colloquial, but generally intelligible– sufficient for *the common person to* make use of it (Lavalle Cobo, 2009). This means that, although technical language may be unattainable for the general public, its translation must respect the rules of adequate semantics to be appropriate for common knowledge.

This issue is problematic because a significant amount of information is presented using highly technical language that can only be understood by specialists. However, the standard requires to ensure that the information is not manipulated by the public administration with the purpose or effect of confusing the petitioner or to conceal the data, thereby making it more challenging for authorities to fulfill their responsibilities. In the realm of environmental law, a precise comprehension of the information presented holds higher relevance. Consequently, the European Parliament has incorporated a requirement for accessibility in its legislation regarding access to environmental information (Pigrau Solé 2008, 97). The Escazú Agreement requires that technical information be adapted before its dissemination so that the public can be *effectively* informed (Article 7.6(a)). This feature is of utmost relevance since it implies that the obligation of the state does not end with the physical (or digital) delivery of the required information, but that, on the contrary, its adequacy to meet the recipient's understanding must be warranted.

Comprehensibility does not simply refer to the language or typography of a document, but to its content being assimilable for the common citizen, so as to ensure that a certain person or community will be able to use it. In this regard, Del Solar (2008) also states that the readability and comprehensibility of information are part of the pro-transparency standard.

In certain circumstances, the information must be translated or interpreted, especially when it is highly technical prior to its proactive dissemination. In addition, the state must help the citizen to understand public information when dealing with minorities, such as people with disabilities or ethnic groups that practice languages different from those of the majority of the population. This may require workshops organized by the state organisms to socialize the information contained in manuals, studies, programs or project descriptions.

Beyond the legal aspects, the importance of language for life in society is indisputable. As a simple example, one of the integration problems suffered by immigrants around the world is the impossibility of expressing themselves in the environment they enter. If it is not guaranteed that a person is reasonably able to understand the information, allowing access to the physical source of the information is not a valid fulfillment of the state's obligations.

Impartiality

Impartiality or objectiveness, although not identical to truthfulness, refers to the reliability of information by ensuring that it is not biased, free from any manipulation of public opinion through its content. According to the Constitutional Court of Ecuador, information is objective when "*the language is axiomatically neutral and devoid of emotional charge. That is, when it is not suggestive and does not seek to manipulate or vitiate consent*"[39].

This characteristic becomes relevant in the context of public decisions that have the potential to affect the livelihoods of communities and future generations. The treatment of information that deviates from objectiveness may occur when the unfavorable aspects of a given state decision are downplayed or its advantages are emphasized. In cases of this nature, the reliability of the information transmitted is reduced, as it tends to align with the outcome intended by the information provider[40]. In any case, a reasonable effort to present the facts fairly is necessary to satisfy this requirement, an effort that must be demonstrable upon request.

---

[39] CONAIE v. MAATE 2023.

[40] Barragan and Sanhueza 2023, 231.

Timeliness: When to Provide Information

Once again, Lavalle Cobo refers to this concept by analyzing its negative effects. According to the author, "*delay may hinder the exercise or enjoyment of other rights or impede the control of the public administration or the fulfillment of the purposes for which it was requested*" (2009, 21).

The UN standards, explains Mendel, require states to "*impose strict time limits for processing requests for information* (2009, 46)." The Council of Europe Recommendations also foresee that requests for access should be processed in a timely manner and within the established timeframe. The Aarhus Convention, on the other hand, establishes that the information must be provided as soon as possible and within a maximum of one month, renewable for another one if the complexity of the information so justifies, which means that the requested authority must demonstrate the need for the extension. In the case of the Escazú Agreement, the response to such request may take thirty working days, extendable in exceptional circumstances for an additional period of ten working days, provided that domestic legislation does not indicate shorter deadlines.

In the case of consumers, the *opportunity* becomes effective if the information is provided in advance, ensuring that the person will be sufficiently informed *before* deciding whether to contract with the supplier, avoiding being induced to rush into contractual bounds that may not be sufficiently clear, and allowing a reasonable period of time to meditate on this matter[41]. This rule becomes relevant in many important business decisions such as health services, insurance, investments and others that may compromise the welfare of a person and his or her estate.

The possibility of processing requests for access to public information must be taken into account not only for the request before the public authority, but also when the request has been denied and the petitioner has to resort to a higher or external body (depending on the legal framework, when the request is submitted to the Ombudsman or other administrative body) or when the judiciary initiates proceedings for the same cause[42]. In addition, timeliness is relevant in terms of the information that state entities must actively publish and disseminate, generally through digital portals. It is important to bear in mind that the provision of information, either upon request or through active dissemination, cannot be interpreted as a favor from the state, but as a citizen's right and a duty of transparency for the

---

[41] Lavalle Cobo 2009, 24.

[42] In Ecuador, the appeal for access to public information has been established as a guarantee of the expeditious exercise of this right (Ecuador. Constituent Assembly 2008, Article 91).

public administration. Consequently, the administration must observe quality standards to *give back* to the public the information that belongs to it.

Relevance: What Information to Deliver

Relevance is a subjective element since it is conditioned by the interests of the people who approach the information. As described above, people's necessity may range from the most urgent to the least socially important purposes. Nevertheless, all requests are equally binding on the state because they all have the same legal protection, since they arise from the fundamental right to information. In addition, the state cannot inquire about the applicant's purpose for accessing the information, so all requests must be met on equal terms. As a consequence, when faced with a specific request, the state cannot decide what information to provide and what to keep for itself.

The criterion is different when dealing with active dissemination by the public offices. The information that the obligated entity actively publishes on its websites, posters, advertising, media, communication campaigns, etc., may not always be what the user or citizen needs to fulfill their various desires and interests. However the broad spectrum, the interests of citizens should be taken into consideration for active dissemination and should prevail when deciding what information to provide. In short, government agencies must make available information that is relevant to citizens, even if it is not popular, i.e., even if it will generate "problems". The dissemination of information serves the purpose of strengthening public debate, so it is clear that it will cause *discomfort* in the public managers, since it may translate into citizen demands. The feature of relevance protects the people from propaganda devoid of objective content. The government must present reality as it is, not as it would suit certain particular interests. Mezones (2006, 35) presents a very illustrative example:

> In general, residents are not interested in knowing how many tons of garbage are collected per week in a city but are more concerned about cleaning up the neighborhood (...). Therefore, asking about progress in quality of life requires us to process information from many sources, going beyond municipal services.

Once more, protection against propaganda and rumors must be taken into account by policy makers. The decision on what information to deliver and how to do it should be taken by the public interest as a matter of priority and not by the convenience of a specific political faction, even if it is the one in power by democratic election. This decision includes a high level of ethics, but beyond that, it must be based on the principle of good faith and objectiveness. To ensure reasonableness in this decision, the information control agency may establish an index or matrix of relevant data that should be disseminated in order to meet this standard.

Finally, the characteristic of relevance also restricts unfair practices, such as sinking the petitioner in a sea of trivial information, thus hiding the really important, *uncomfortable* data. From a formal point of view, the state would be compliant by delivering a tower of unsystematized documents. However, by violating the rule of relevance, the custodian of the information may be held liable for not providing it in a truly useful form.

Accessibility: How to Deliver Information

Accessibility of information means making it possible for citizens to acquire it easily, which, among other things, means establishing mechanisms for indexing and cross-referencing data, so that efficient searches and aggregations are possible and user-defined searches are available, without relying solely on the authority's criteria[43].

Communication, as stated above, is a two-part process and a channel through which a message passes from one patrimony of knowledge to another. Accessibility refers to the channel or medium that transmits the information, requiring that it be suitable for the citizen to receive it. Mezones considers that "*the mechanisms for organizing and retrieving information are essential*" (2006, 36). The question brings us back to the simple administrative acts consisting of data filing and processing, which must be aimed at ensuring the most appropriate way for the citizen to obtain the data of interest to him or her.

The Aarhus Convention imposes on states the process of indexing environmental information, which is often voluminous. This international treaty also gives citizens the possibility of choosing the medium in which they wish to receive the information, so that it is easy to study, in addition to economic factors that must be considered as well.

Accessibility involves the economic factor, from where international regulations tend to establish free services to deliver the information produced by the public administration, urging states to charge only the costs of reproduction. See the feature of *gratuity* for more on this subject.

---

[43] Abramo 2002, cited by Mezones 2006, 36.

EXCEPTIONS REGIME

The right to information is not unlimited: it allows for restrictions to prevent or deal with conflicts with other fundamental interests that may interfere with the purpose of this right, and which also require protection under the laws enforced by government authorities, who have a social responsibility toward the fulfillment of all human rights. To avoid the primacy of one right from leading to the infringement of another, it is necessary to establish exceptions that restrict public access to certain information. Such exceptions must be consistent with international treaties, as well as with legal principles and the decisions of international courts, and the interpretative focus of human rights commissions. They should also be consistent with national legislation, public policies and the local administration of justice. The application of these exclusions must be proportional, meaning that they should be appropriate to the intended purpose, with meticulous vigilance to prevent any abuse and to maintain transparency and access to information of public interest as an essential element of the democratic state.

In addition, it is crucial to educate public officials –especially, but not only them, but society in general– about the broadest possible exercise of this right without overstepping the boundaries of privacy and the protection of other needs of the population. The aim is to avoid unjustified damage to the private life and reputation of individuals, as well as the disclosure of data that could endanger national security or the functions of vital state institutions. In essence, the control of information as a fundamental right must be balanced and adaptable, taking into the analysis the specific wants and circumstances of each community, while maintaining the fundamental values of transparency and the protection of human rights. It is important to bear in mind that legislation is guided by the principles of progressivity and prohibition of regression, which are established globally through human rights instruments, having clear examples in the Americas, Europe and Africa. Accordingly, it is up to the states to maintain systems in which both the protection of private and family life and access to information of public relevance coexist.

Thus, exceptions must cover all possible cases and, in some legal systems, can only be formulated through laws passed by Parliament. This ensures that no subordinate norm, such as a resolution of a public institution, a general regulation, an ordinance or a public policy, may reduce the content or scope of the right of access to public information. Allowing this would be practically taking power away from the norm that guarantees access because each public institution or authority would impose its own catalog of exceptions, as it sees fit. This legal concept is called "reserve of law" and plays an important role in safeguarding the right of access to public information because it provides a higher level of certainty and sufficient predictability for the citizen. In short, in a democracy, as opposed to an inquisitorial state, public actions are transparent by default, with exceptions strictly governed by law. This is utterly explained by UNESCO:

> In summary, regarding the right to access to public documents, international law establishes a general principle according to which the right to access public information is the rule and nondisclosure the exception. This exception can only be legitimate if it complies with the requirements imposed, in general, by Article 19.3 of the ICCPR[44]. Accordingly, restrictions to the right to access public information must have been established by law, serve a legitimate objective and be necessary, which in turn requires that they be intended to satisfy a compelling public interest (UNESCO 2021, 84).

Acceptable restrictions to the right of access to public information, according to their nature, are classified into those of public interest and those of private interest, as will be seen below.

Personal Data Protection

The controversy over the processing of personal data, protected by the right to respect private and family life, is not a central theme of this study, but it is essential to emphasize that these two rights (access and concealment) are intrinsically interconnected because both have at their core *information* as the object of a *fundamental* human right. Both have equal legal value, given their nature, and in both cases information is held in a public repository. The protection of personal data and access to public information are equal obligations of states. Consequently, the American Convention and the European Convention, in very similar terms, protect personal information

[44] Article 19.3 [Freedom of Expression] The exercise of the rights provided for in paragraph 2 of this article carries with it special duties and responsibilities. It may therefore be subject to certain restrictions, but these shall only be such as are provided by law and are necessary:
(a) For respect of the rights or reputations of others;
(b) For the protection of national security or of public order (ordre public), or of public health or morals

within their respective regions. The European Convention establishes the right to the preservation of private and family existence. Similarly, the American Convention guarantees the right to privacy, which encompasses protection against unfair and detrimental intrusion into one's personal and family existence:

European Convention on Human Rights, Article 8	American Convention on Human Rights, Article 11
Right to respect for private and family life 1. Everyone has the right to respect for his private and family life, his home and his correspondence. 2. There shall be no interference by a public authority with the exercise of this right except such as is in accordance with the law and is necessary in a democratic society in the interests of national security, public safety or the economic well-being of the country, for the prevention of disorder or crime, for the protection of health or morals, or for the protection of the rights and freedoms of others.	**Right to Privacy** 1. Everyone has the right to have his honor respected and his dignity recognized. 2. No one may be the object of arbitrary or abusive interference with his private life, his family, his home or his correspondence, or of unlawful attacks on his honor or reputation. 3. Everyone has the right to the protection of the law against such interference or attacks.

Concomitantly, both regional courts (the American and the European) have determined that this right protects personal information, data and records, i.e., the entire continent and content related to the private life of individuals.

The analysis of these two articles leads us to some important conclusions that cannot be left without comment: on one side, both conventions identify the elements of privacy as: private life, family, home and correspondence. Both conventions also guarantee the protection of honor and reputation (in the case of the European Convention, in Article 10). On the other side, it is clear that the right to privacy also has limits (similar, by the way, to the limits applicable to the accessibility of information): (i) according to the European Convention: national security, the economic well-being of the country, the prevention of crime and disorder, the protection of health and morals, the right of others; (ii) according to these conventions, only the law may authorize interference in private life, interdicting arbitrariness and abuse of state power. Alongside, as summarized by Vianna (2010, 185), keeping personal data secret requires that the management techniques of such information be made public and transparent:

> The private opacity that ensures the confidentiality of personal records can only be guaranteed if public transparency of the activities of monitoring and processing of secret personal data is made effective.

Personal information is restricted from the public sphere to the extent that (i) it is related to personal and family privacy or (ii) it presents a discriminatory potential, as consolidated by Upegui (2020). The Ecuadorian Constitution provides an exemplary list of criteria suspicious of discrimination, compiling those developed by supranational jurisprudence, particularly those of the Inter-American Court. These include sex, gender identity, political affiliation, HIV status, health condition, among others, and is drafted as an open clause, including any permanent or temporary distinction that leads to a different treatment before the law. Argentine jurisprudence also justifies the protection of personal data to save people from the invasion of their intimate life by third parties with the power to cause serious and systematic damage:

> The sad experiences of ideological persecution lived in the country fully justify the protection –through the action of habeas data– of information related to political affiliation, religious beliefs, union militancy, or performance in the labor or academic field, among many other data referring to the person entitled to the right, which should not be available to the public or be used by public bodies or private entities, without any right to support its use (Gozaíni 2006, 168).

But personal information also includes nominal criteria such as age, marital status or place of birth, which are personal but public data, easily accessible by third parties without any authorization from the owner. Hence Upegui (2020) calls the term "sensitive personal information" a "*niche of paradoxes*" that complicates its legal handling. In any case –and demonstrating how unfinished the subject is– "*if it is a general rule that all personal information is confidential, sensitive personal information will be all the more* so"[45], concludes the author. He also recalls that the right to the protection of personal data is triggered when there is an unjustified interference with an individual's privacy, according to the jurisprudential development of the European Court of Justice. In this case, too, a balancing test is required to determine whether such interference is justified by a higher and valid purpose according to the human rights charters. Thus, once again, we are faced with a system that requires a case-by-case assessment in which the norms and theory only show a (perfectible, undoubtedly) direction and not definitive solutions.

---

[45] Upegui Mejía 2020, 304.

Therefore, in situations where these rights conflict –i.e., the right to access public information versus the right to privacy– it is mandatory for states to carefully consider both fundamental aspects and balance the importance of disclosing information set against protecting it from public access, in order to make a decision appropriate to each specific case. There are no exact recipes but there are principles that guide state action. Consider, for example, an individual suffering from cancer who seeks to find out the technological capabilities of the nearby public hospital to treat this disease. It should be noted that such an individual is not obliged to disclose personal data concerning her or himself or their medical condition in order to gain access to information from that public hospital. On the contrary, individuals will be prohibited from accessing this patient's medical records, which are stored in the public hospital, even though they are generated by a government institution, with the exception of anonymous statistical data (which must be disclosed). Therefore, in the context of requests seeking access to public information, it is not mandatory to establish a connection between the information and the requester. This is because the application in question cannot include any personal data, which is subject to other legislative regulations. In short, it is necessary to point out that any personal data that derives from fundamental rights and has the potential to infringe a citizen's right to privacy must be protected and kept confidential, ensuring that it remains out of the public domain and the entities associated with this right. But this does not preclude any public data from being disclosed upon citizen request or as required by law to be actively disseminated.

However, the scope of these rights may become ambiguous, particularly in cases where conflicting interests or interpretations arise. Authorities, including the courts, must weigh the right to access public information, to inform and be informed, and the right to privacy and protection of personal data. The assessment must be carried out on the basis of the relevant facts of every particular case, as none of these seemingly conflicting rights are unconditional and allow for restrictions in relation to public order. The guiding principles provided for in international instruments and the theory of the right of access to public information are increasingly relevant to this type of dispute. The principle of maximum disclosure requires states to comply strictly with the exceptions provided by law prior to the request for access, and to ensure that any section of the requested data that is deemed public is provided to the petitioner. In the European context, the Magyar Helsinki Bizottsag v. Hungary (2016) case addressed this issue, recognizing that while the right to protection of personal data is important in certain circumstances, it does not trump the public's right to access such information when it comes to public scrutiny of specific administrative proceedings, in that instance, in relation to the performance of public defenders. The court was forced to address the conflict between legitimate public interest and the protection of privacy, among other important factors. In this case, the ECrtHR concluded that, when assessed on an individual basis, certain personal information may acquire importance in the formation of public sentiment and, therefore, be properly disclosed in accordance with Article 10 of the European Convention:

> [The concept of privacy] Covers the physical and psychological integrity of a person. It can therefore embrace multiple aspects of a person's physical and social identity. Elements such as, for example, gender identification, name and sexual orientation and sexual life fall within the personal sphere protected by Article 8 (see S. and Marper, cited above, § 66, and Pretty, cited above, § 61, with further references). Private life may also include activities of a professional or business nature (see Niemietz v. Germany, 16 December 1992, § 29, Series A no. 251-B). The Court has also held that there is a zone of interaction of a person with others, even in a public context, which may fall within the scope of "private life" (see Couderc and Hachette Filipacchi Associés, cited above, § 83).

In Magyar Helsinki Bizottsag v. Hungary, the information requested consisted of the names of public defenders and the number of times they had been appointed as attorneys in certain jurisdictions, in order to assess whether there was a bias in the assignment of public defenders and their performance in favor of their defendants, which could be contrary to judicial protection, and to the right to a fair trial. According to the ECrtHR, the request for the list of names, number of cases and proceedings, although constituting personal data, predominantly refers to the performance of professional activities in the context of a public proceeding. In that context, the professional activities of public defenders could not be considered as a private matter[46]. In the end, the Court granted access to the required data.

According to Uicich (1999), the search for personal information in the exercise of the right to information is incompatible with the right of access to public information, from a purely theoretical point of view. This is because the primary objective of this right is to expose government actions to the public, rather than to deprive individuals of their intimate lives. This perspective is supported by the cited Magyar Helsinki Bizottsag v. Hungary case, which disentangled the public importance of the required information in the face of the potential *sensitivity* of the private data comprised in it. Moreover, to the extent that the data of the person in question lacks practical relevance in relation to the exercise of the political, social or environmental

[46] Magyar Helsinki Bizottsag v. Hungary 2016, parr. 191, 194.

rights of the petitioner or the community, it is understood that these belong specifically to the sphere of his or her private life. Thus, the scope of the right to privacy encompasses parts of life that facilitate the development of an individual's character and life project, specifically, those that are within the autonomy of the individual.

The right to privacy legally protects an area of individual autonomy constituted by feelings, beliefs, ideology, habits, customs, family relationships, economic situation, religious beliefs, mental and physical health and, in short, actions, facts or data, which, pertaining the ways of life accepted by the community, are reserved for the individual. Disclosure of the same to strangers pose an actual or potential threat to privacy and even to personal security and integrity.

In a similar vein, the Inter-American Law Model (OAS, 2020) specifies that the level of private protection granted to public officials decreases inversely to the increase in their responsibilities within the government structure. In fact, it establishes an objective monetary threshold to define the term "senior official"[47]. This parameter is invaluable when information is required on a particular authority, his or her assets and even specific private actions, such as associations with third parties that call into question the legitimacy of that authority's decisions and even connections with illegal groups. The conclusion here is: when dealing with actions carried out in the exercise of public power, the public interest prevails. Therefore, it is legitimate for civil society (including the media or investigators) to scrutinize the highest government authorities that can dismantle collusive and even criminal actions, always limited to the exercise of their public functions and the external forces that can influence them.

This question is not a simple one. Often, public scrutiny looks for clues about a senior official's character in his or her private behavior. In 1998, Bill Clinton was called by the U.S. House of Representatives to testify about the existence of an inappropriate sexual relationship with a subordinate, Monica Lewinsky. The case produced a scandal of planetary dimensions and had a great impact on Clinton's life, Hilary Clinton's, Al Gore's and his presidential expectations, as well as on Lewinsky and her professional career. There are a number of edges from which this case can be approached, but one of them is the way in which the boundary between what is publicly relevant and what is not is thinned when a person is in the exercise of a popular mandate. One can argue that a person's sex life is not definitive evidence of his or her ability to honestly manage the *res publica.* But the

[47] Article 1: Definitions. In this Act, unless the context otherwise requires (...) "Senior Officials" refers to any official within a Public Authority whose total annual salary exceeds USD$100,000.

counterargument is strongly grounded too. For Owen Fiss (2008), today's democratic societies have placed public authorities in a kind of reverse panopticon in which society can scrutinize even the most intimate aspects of the politician, but not vice versa, and this requires the highest level of visibility:

> In most cases, the decision to endow an individual with discretionary power should, to a large extent, arouse our interest in the individual's character assessment, as this is the most reliable indication of how his or her power will be used. The information related to character assessments is limitless; almost every aspect of a person's life, even the most intimate, such as family relationships, has a bearing on character (Fiss 2008, 314).

In addition, those who run for public office do so knowing that they assume greater exposure and that their activities, once private, become of interest to the community. In other words, it is a risk consciously assumed when accepting such an assignment[48]. The turning point is that transparency in the public sphere goes beyond legal technicalities. It plays a transcendental role in democracy and fosters a culture against corruption and prone to public ethics. To that extent, it is related to the sustainability of the state itself and of the services necessary for the advancement and realization of human rights.

However, the protection of personal data is becoming a right in its own, gaining autonomy over the right to privacy. The current context of the information society, of a life that increasingly takes place in a virtual ecosystem so that practically every person on the planet has an ethereal *personality* composed of data, requires a commensurate level of protection. In this sense, states have a specific mandate in relation to personal information: to prevent unauthorized access to and dissemination of information pertaining to the privacy of the individual. This right is realized, like any fundamental right, through negative obligations (respect) and positive obligations (protection and guarantee). In this case, public entities are obliged to adopt physical and electronic security measures to ensure that the information will not be subject to theft, robbery or criminal access and modification. Likewise, public officials must maintain the confidentiality of this information and not disseminate or abuse it. This can be highly relevant in sensitive matters such as judicial past, political affiliation or even patrimonial information. Think, for example, of the amount of personal data held by tax administrations and its importance for the development of an individual's character or personality, as well as for the security of the

[48] Fiss 2008, 321.

individual and his or her family. Knowing the amount of money, assets and location of a person is clearly highly sensitive. Its commercial and economic implications can constitute privileged information that puts certain individuals in a position to *abuse* it. Therefore, the handling of this data requires a high degree of ethics and summons for proper public policies. Therefore, the right to the protection of personal data includes:

> (...) the principle of purpose, which includes the prohibition of processing personal data for illegitimate purposes or purposes other than those communicated to the owner, including, for example, indiscriminate advertising; and the principle of security, which includes the adoption of physical and technical security measures, not only to prevent unauthorized access, but also to ensure the availability of the information for the purposes for which it was collected (...). (Upegui Mejía 2020, 326).

Thus, the right to the protection of personal data applies to the data that has been hosted on public platforms by decision of the owner or as determined by law. Thence, the discussion on privacy is less relevant since the level of protection of personal data is objective and specific. It is not necessary to prove the origin of the information (it is already known beforehand that it is *personal* information) as it happens in the assessment of a case of private life information of public relevance. It is sufficient that the information falls within the definition of "personal data" for it to be subject to state protection.

As Abramovich and Courtis (2000) point out, the availability of personal data in the databases of public agencies can serve as an important mechanism for monitoring the actions of investigative agencies, such as the police or the military. This is especially relevant because of the possibility of these agencies engaging in excessive and abusive exercise of their authority. These authors believe that being aware of the presence of personal data in the databases of state surveillance and control agencies will prevent their misuse and promote regular updates. However, the implementation of biocontrol measures is very sensitive and may not be perfectly in line with the principles of a democratic society. At the end of the day, the *dangerousness,* the level of *risk,* or what is considered *normal*, will be defined by whoever holds power and this comes along a huge responsibility that can hardly be absent of abuses[49]. Hence, it is imperative to *watch the watchers*. It is

[49] On this point, Vianna (2010, 130-131) offers his perspective: Systems can be programmed to filter individuals by any of these characteristics [names, judicial past, ethnicity, religion, sexual orientation, political militancy and so many other sensitive data] or by certain combinations of them. There are no technological limits to the

therefore mandatory for public ofices to exercise the utmost caution when dealing with a substantial volume of nominal data stored in both public and private databases. One should not lose sight of the fact that the right to privacy is, in addition to being constitutional, inviolable by nature.

The right of access to information is not a license to undermine other rights that protect human dignity. The right to honor and reputation may conflict with the entitlement to obtain information. Reputation is acknowledged as an intangible asset in different settings, such as social, family life, with the ability to be assigned a monetary value in business and other contexts of economic life. Even more, it is widely acknowledged by both national and international courts that reputation, public image, and good name are commonly considered valuable assets that warrant legal protection and financial compensation when unlawfully harmed. Fiss brings up a case that illustrates this point precisely:

> Neither freedom of speech nor freedom of the press are absolute concepts. We tolerate restrictions on speech and the press, although we require that they be examined with strict scrutiny and confined to a narrow scope. For example, in the New York Times v. Sullivan case decided in 1964, the U.S. Supreme Court declared the constitutional possibility of defamation actions and imposed limitations on defamation. In this case, the Court ruled that public servants could be compensated for damages if their reputation was affected by a newspaper article provided that: 1) the damage was due to a statement of fact as opposed to the expression of an opinion; 2) the statement of fact was false; 3) the reporter or broadcaster knew or had good reason to know that the statement was false. The limitations imposed by the Court restricted defamation actions to deliberate lies and reckless falsehoods, based on the theory that the press needs "breathing room" to fulfill its democratic mission, which, of course, is to provide citizens with all the information they need to effectively govern (Fiss 2008, 318).

For Fiss, from the perspective of a press that is functional to a democratic purpose –after all, they fulfill a traditional role of being the watchdogs of democracy–, restrictions on the dissemination of information cannot be such as to restrict the flow of communication to the citizenry. Then, defamatory messages, according to the commented ruling, are only subject to review when there is a purpose to mislead the recipients of the message. Hence, it would be required to prove that the sender or media was aware of the falsity

---

definition of these filters, which can be freely created according to the convenience of the dominant power (...).

of what was transmitted. However, if there are gray lines[50], there is no room for such restrictions because it would be contrary to the right to information by preventing the formation of a critical opinion in the citizenship. This notion must be compatible with the absence of protection of messages lacking veracity and aimed at manipulating public opinion.

In tandem, the reputation of an individual or an organization that provides public services or is subject to public scrutiny cannot limit access to sources that include data of public importance. Consider, for instance, the number of legal proceedings related to medical malpractice cases that a doctor faces. Despite the potential for substantial harm to his or her professional status, the prerogative of prospective patients to opt for treatment with that health care provider or an alternative one trumps the physician's right to maintain his or her professional integrity.

But there is another side to this openness: the existence of legal procedures directed at children and adolescents can have detrimental consequences for their reputation, public perception and prospects in their adult life. In this specific case, the child's right to privacy also protects his or her right to develop a life project free of prejudice and therefore prevails over the interest that the general public may have in knowing about his or her judicial past. As such, the Beijing Rules explicitly remove judicial proceedings initiated against minors from public exposure to protect their privacy and prevent possible damage to their reputation in order to ensure their integration into society on an equal footing with their peers –at least from the perspective of the judicial past.

Trade Secret and Other Protected Data

Not only physical persons are guaranteed their right to honor. In legal or fictitious persons, the right to a good name is guaranteed too. The scope of protection shelters the set of attributes that allow them to develop a function in society, whether it is economic, altruistic, scientific, sporting, educational, etc. The right to a good name is developed in a similar way to the right to honor of physical persons and is subject to the same limitations. Likewise, in the event that these legal entities perform public functions or act under state delegation, the information corresponding to the state capital or to the public function or service may not be treated as personal information and

[50] For contrast, Fiss (2008, 319-320) cites Time, Inc. v. Hill in which a family, made a public figure though not connected to public administration, had a serious fact of their private life exposed and misrepresented by Life magazine, in which the Supreme Court held that there was no right to damages because the magazine did not know that the information it had conveyed was untrue.

must be delivered and disseminated according to the common rules of public information. However, citizens may not demand access to proprietary information that constitutes a professional secret or is subject to other types of protection.

All the standards analyzed in this study take into consideration the information developed within companies and organizations aimed at their protection and removal from the public sphere. While an interest may be claimed in certain types of information of this kind (consider, for example, a drug that cures a complex disease), the parameters for disclosure safeguard the interests of the developer, author or other rights holders in connection with such information.

The right to benefit from the moral recognition of the works produced by one's intellect is embodied in Article 27.2 of the Universal Declaration of Human Rights and other international instruments. But another type of recognition inherent to intellectual inventions is of an economic nature. The World Intellectual Property Organization ("WIPO") administers a series of international treaties that protect the creations of human ingenuity so that their commercial exploitation corresponds to their legitimate holders or owners. Among the international treaties relating to the protection of intellectual property, the Paris Convention and the Agreement on Trade-Related Aspects of Intellectual Property Rights of the World Trade Organization ("TRIPS"), which expressly refers to the Paris Convention, stand out. These instruments clarify that intellectual property rights are, by nature, private, although their use for the benefit of mankind is recognized, without ignoring the ownership of the creators. The set of international treaties on intellectual property –which derive to the domestic legislation of the states the regulation of the matter– are aimed at protecting copyrights and related rights, trademarks, industrial designs, patents, layout-designs of integrated circuits, as well as other forms of inventive creation that may be susceptible of appropriation. In TRIPS, secrecy (or undisclosed information) is an autonomous category of intellectual property with a regime of protection, in the first instance, from misappropriation by third parties. And, in the second instance, it demands that each state guarantees that data submitted to governments for public filings, authorizations and such, will be kept confidential. Article 39 proposes rules that exclude the appropriation of knowledge by third parties:

1. It must be secret in the sense that people who are usually involved in the specific field of knowledge would not be able to acquire it on their own.
2. The fact that it is secret should give the information a commercial value.
3. The legitimate owner of the information must take reasonable measures to keep such information secret.

In attention to this specific group of human rights, international and domestic legislation prevents abuses through limiting access and stating confidentiality obligations on the states. The Inter-American Law Model (OAS, 2020, Article 32) defines the private interests to be protected and therefore, any request for access may be denied if it concerns legitimate commercial and economic interests. Accordingly, the internal rules of the states eliminate from public access information considered to be of a private nature and for private commercial exploitation, protected by industrial secrecy:

	Legal body	**Provisions on Commercial Secrets and Similar Information**
Argentina	Law No. 27275 Right to Access Public Information, article 8	*Exceptions.* The regulated entities may only be exempted from providing the information in the following cases: (...) c) Industrial, commercial, financial, scientific, technical or technological secrets, the disclosure of which could damage the level of competitiveness or harm the interests of the regulated entity.
Ecuador	Organic law of transparency and access to public information, article 5	Confidential Information: Information or documentation, in any format, final or preparatory, whether or not it has been generated by the obligated subject, derived from the personal and personal rights and and requires the express authorization of its owner for its disclosure, which contains fundamental data, and which which, if disclosed, could harm the following private interests: (...) c) Legitimate commercial and economic interests; and, d) Patents, copyrights and trade secrets.

Mexico	Federal law of transparency and access to public information, article 113.	The following is considered confidential information: (...) Banking, fiduciary, industrial, commercial, commercial, tax, stock exchange and postal secrets, whose ownership corresponds to individuals, subjects of international law or regulated entities when they do not involve the use of public resources.
United Kingdom	Freedom Information Act 2000, article 43	Commercial interests. (1)Information is exempt information if it constitutes a trade secret. (2)Information is exempt information if its disclosure under this Act would, or would be likely to, prejudice the commercial interests of any person (including the public authority holding it).

However, it should not be lost sight of the fact that certain information, in principle private, characterized by having been gathered or produced without direct state intervention, may still be considered public if its manager acts under concession or delegation of the state (provided that the local law enables so). It is appropriate, once again, to refer to the case of Claude Reyes v. Chile (2006), because it showed that in such cases the public interest prevails over nondisclosure, which acquires greater legal weight than the duty to protect private information under certain circumstances. Therefore, the IACrtHR ruled that, although the data requested by the journalists had been collected in the context of a private project, the owner of the information would be acting under a state permit in an activity with a significant impact on the environment due to the forestry industrialization it implied. Claude Reyes' request included financial background of the foreign company investing in the project, the suitability of the investor and the seriousness of the investment offer, as well as certain public information. There is an evident collision between these two principles at the highest level. In such a predicament, a case-by-case approach is advisable.

Genetic Material

Scientific research is protected by freedom of thought and is oriented to improving the quality of life of mankind. However, scientific progress can always be controversial and raise ethical questions. Careful handling of genetic information is required to protect the privacy of the individuals involved as well as their dignity, since human experimentation is prohibited because it violates the fundamental principle that the human being is an end in itself and should not be objectified. Moreover, genetic modification for commercial purposes, even if not on humans, compromises integrity. States, especially developed ones, face a very important moral challenge regarding the handling of genetic material and its connection to the right to development, privacy and well-being of individuals.

According to Article 5 (b) of the United Nations Declaration on the Human Genome, the decision on research, treatment or diagnosis related to the genome requires the prior, free and informed consent of the individual. Nevertheless, scientific research on the subject is respected within the framework defined by human dignity and the other rights recognized to physical persons, and a call is made to ethics and to direct research towards the alleviation of diseases and the improvement of the health conditions of humankind.

The issue of genetic material, its treatment and ownership has had asymmetric approaches in Europe and Latin America. For the European Union, according to Directive 98/44/EC, isolated elements of the human body, such as the partial sequence of a gene, can be considered a patentable invention, but it excludes:

> (...) the patentability of an invention when the technical information that is the subject of the patent application requires the prior destruction of human embryos or their use as raw material;
>
> (…) the patentability in relation with the utilization of human embryos with industrial or commercial ends (Guillem-Tatay 2012, 49).

This shows that, in the European circuit, the limit has been drawn as soon as the biotechnological invention threatens human embryos.

For the Andean Community of Nations, the possibility of patenting or registering, as a product of human intellect, all or part of living beings, including biological material existing in nature, the genome and germplasm of all living beings, is completely excluded[51].

In Ecuador, information related to one's own genetic material is considered private information whose owner would be the person to whom such material belongs, in accordance with the National Constitution (Article 92). However, genetic material belonging to non-human beings is considered of public interest and a strategic sector (Articles 313, 400). In this regard, the Ecuadorian Constitution prohibits the use of genetic material when it violates human rights (Article 66), and likewise prohibits the private

[51] Sacoto 2023, 14.

appropriation of the country's genetic patrimony in relation to biological diversity and agro-biodiversity (Article 322). In addition, the national genetic heritage is protected by prohibiting the introduction of organisms and organic or inorganic material that may irreversibly alter it (Article 73).

Trade Secret

Information pertaining to intellectual development is not the only form of secrecy that is recognized as exceeding the regime of public information. Professional secrecy, of long standing, is also considered a basic human right since it enables several fundamental rights and freedoms, such as the right not to incriminate oneself, the free development of personality, freedom of conscience, freedom of enterprise, among others. In Argentina[52] and in the United Kingdom[53], the corresponding laws on access to public information explicitly exclude professional secrecy from the universe of information accessible to the public, while in other states its protection is provided for in various bodies of law, thus confirming the practically universal nature of this legal value. The most elementary example of this type of secrecy is the communication between the client and the lawyer. Although the debate on this right had apparently been overcome, it has been recently reopened in view of the participation of legal and financial advisors in the commission of crimes of an economic nature. In several types of crimes against public confidence in financial systems, it has been discovered that the role of advisors has not been limited to providing legitimate ways to solve problems, but they have actively participated in the consolidation of structures to defraud third parties, including states' treasuries. So how far does attorney-client confidentiality go and where does active criminal liability on the part of the counselor begin? This is a clear case of conflict between the public's interest in knowing the reality of transactions and structures, in principle private and kept confidential by the advisors involved in their creation, in front of transparency in financial management that may affect markets and even peoples. Hence, in certain legislations, financial services are considered private but of public interest and are therefore highly regulated by control entities. For Irma Sandoval (2008, 206), transparency and accountability in the financial sector, and more so in the public sector, is essential for the effectiveness of the organizations that manage the country's resources. To demonstrate this, she cites the Geraats standards on transparency categories that should be applied to central banks:

[52] Argentina. Senate and Chamber of Deputies 2016, article 8 (c).
[53] Parliament of the United Kingdom 2022, article 42.

- Policy: on the bank's objectives and its relationship with the government.
- Economic: indicators and projections.
- Procedures: on how decisions are made.
- Policies: the bank's strategies and any changes to them.
- Operations: internal functioning of the bank.

Sandoval concludes that transparency in the economic management of a country is unavoidable because opacity "*is an ideal breeding ground for the development of moral hazard*", and she maintains that:

> It is imperative to guarantee full access to and disclosure of information related to the management of financial and monetary variables. This implies that the information handled by the entities that make up the country's financial institutional framework cannot be indiscriminately classified as reserved (...) What really damages the economic or financial stability of a nation is not transparency and accountability but opacity and secrecy in the management of public resources and affairs; it is necessary to break away from the conceptions that confuse technocracy with opacity or impunity.

Finance and data are practically the same thing in the information age. Money *is digital*; what a country, a company or a person *owns* is what is displayed on a computer screen. Therefore, transparency in the management of funds on which the state and social structure is based –here, the distinction between public and private assets takes a secondary place– will have a direct impact on risk containment, on the detection of abuses and on the application of corrective measures to avoid new bursts such as the real estate bubble of 2008. Therefore, it is inconceivable to argue that banks are private entities to keep their information absolutely shielded; the public must be able to count on the fact that every asset that depends on any given financial institution is safe and correctly handled.

A case that proves the public interest colliding with professional secret is "Panama Papers", in which the leakage of information protected by professional secrecy made it possible to unravel multimillion-dollar structures used for money laundering and tax evasion. The Parliamentary Assembly of the Council of Europe[54] shows how this case and professional secrecy collide in a way that is detrimental to public opinion and the legitimate interests of third parties who have been defrauded of their taxes:

> In April 2016, an unparalleled leak of information, named the "Panama Papers", caught the attention of the whole world. The documents from the

[54] Parliamentary Assembly of the Council of Europe, 2016.

> database of the world's fourth biggest offshore law firm, Mossack Fonseca, provided "behind the scenes" information on how wealthy people disguise their financial assets in order to avoid tax scrutiny (...)
>
> The recent outcome of the national trial following the LuxLeaks demonstrates the appalling lack of protection for whistle-blowers. The LuxLeaks revelations shed light on hundreds of controversial tax deals granted by the Luxembourg tax office, including tax arrangements helping 340 big companies such as Burberry, Pepsi, Ikea, Heinz, Shire Pharmaceuticals and others, to minimize their tax payments. Following a long trial process, the whistle-blower received a 12-month suspended sentence and was fined €1 500. He was found guilty on charges including theft and violating Luxembourg's strict professional secrecy laws. (...)
>
> Meanwhile, Switzerland's famous banking secrecy law of 1934 was triggered by a French tax-evasion scandal involving several wealthy elites. Thus, since their very creation, tax havens were designed to shield the money of wealthy and powerful people (Explanatory memorandum by Mr Stefan, Schennach, rapporteur).

Evidently, the public interest in certain information causes important tensions on the right to professional secrecy which, in addition, is dual because its holders are both the sender of the message and the receiver. And to make the issue even more complex, this legal institute has gained relevance when it comes to the protection of those who depend on this right to exercise other legitimate rights in a context of security. In 2022, the UN Human Rights Council addressed the Report of the Special Rapporteur on the independence of judges and lawyers, which recognized that lawyers are more vulnerable in the context of fight against corruption and enforcing human rights:

> (...) when its activity is oriented to the fight against corruption, the defense of human rights, women's rights, the protection of ethnic, racial, religious or national minorities, indigenous peoples, LGBTQI+ people, environment or other issues of public relevance (García-Sayán, 2022, para. 2).

The Special Rapporteur describes modern examples of violation of what he calls the "principle of attorney-client privilege" and how this undermines due process, a pillar of the adversarial justice system. According to the report, attorney-client privilege was breached to use intercepted information in court, in Belgium, Romania, France, Russia, including in the context of the COVID-19 pandemic and taking advantage of the constraints it created[55].

For another part, the provision of medical services highlights the importance of extracting patients' data from public knowledge, and even from state bodies. Not only to protect patients from discrimination when their health condition may cause stigma, persecution and exclusion, but also in making decisions about the patient's life, health and body. In the case of De la Cruz Flores v. Peru heard by the IACrtHR, it was established that states cannot criminally prosecute physicians and other health care providers for refraining from disclosing information about punishable conduct of their patients, such as abortion or euthanasia or even participation in acts classified as crimes, the product of which require medical attention (precisely the case of De la Cruz). The reasoned vote of Judge Garcia Ramirez considers that physicians cannot be compelled by the state to assume a role that does not correspond to their profession, such as to become an investigator or informer of the conditions that preceded the victim to seek health assistance[56].

In summary, the protection of professional secrecy is also in the public interest because it is closely linked to the exercise of other human rights such as life, liberty or due process. But when this is opposed to public interests like public ethics and probity, it can produce an imbalance that is difficult to readjust because it can mean assuming a vigilante position that is highly dubious in terms of respect for the law and the protection of human rights. Due to that, more than ever, the need to weigh the legal interests at stake is in order, to draw up (through an objective and proportional exercise) a solution tailored to the case, but always respectful of human rights. It is not an easy task and a mistake can consume an entire population, but it is a necessary exercise and the only one on the horizon for justice to prevail.

Public Interest Exceptions

The international treaties that deal with access to public information emphasize that the acts and facts of public activity that can be excluded from the view of the citizenry can only be limited to those regarding the security of the state, public order, public health or public morals. These constraints align with the restrictions imposed by European and American covenants on freedom of expression. As this right encompasses the ability to acquire or pursue information, namely access to public information (particularly within the Inter-American context), the same limitations are applicable. On

---

[55] García-Sayán, 2022, paras. 95-99.

[56] Cabera & Hevia, 2009.

the issue of morality, since it is eminently of a subjective and cultural kind, the possibility of restricting communication under this justification has been reduced to the point of excluding mainly those messages of hate, apology of crime or discrimination, and those that are inappropriate for children and adolescents. However, in relation to the other points, there is a broader and unfinished development.

Given that the states have been urged to establish limitative lists of exceptions (since the general rule is transparency), the public interest exceptions are broad but similar to each other in the legislations compared in this study. Thus, specific blocks of information that are considered excluded from the public access regime can be identified in each country's own law on access to public information[57], without prejudice to the fact that there may be other rules that allow certain information to be kept secret or confidential in other legal bodies:

	Argentina	**Ecuador**	**Mexico**	**United Kingdom**
National Defense (outside borders)	✓	✓	✓	✓
National Security (within borders)	✓	✓	-	✓
International Relations and Policy	-	✓	✓	✓
Classified Information	✓	✓	✓	According to Government Security Classification Policy
State Economy, Monetary and Financial Policy or Affairs	-	-	✓	✓
Audit and Control	Supervision of financial entities.		✓	✓

[57] All the legislations analyzed here include commercial and industrial secrecy and other forms of protection of private interests in the list of exceptions, which have been dealt with in the section on Personal Data.

Financial and banking system	✓	-	✓	
Court Records	-	Only in cases of sexual violence, children's justice and offending adolescents.	Only until the proceedings are finalized.	✓
Investigation of the Judiciary	✓	-	✓	-
Formulation of government policy, parliamentary procedures and similar	-	Participation of the people in government policy is constitutionally guaranteed.	✓	✓

One of the main functions of the state today is the internal and external protection of borders, citizens and their assets. Beyond the warlike character or the level of violence that characterizes some states in particular, what is certain is that the protection of borders and the guarantee of social peace are indispensable for social and economic development. Due to this, the government is assigned the legitimate use of force. Strategies to meet these challenges cannot be disclosed because they would lack any effectiveness. So, excluding defense and national security information from public access, at least for an appropriate amount of time, is inevitable. But, in any case, the need for internal and external protection and defense cannot promote a climate of defenselessness and abuse of power. In this regard, the UN constantly warns that the rules that allow the limitation of the public on the exercise of power and force deserve special attention:

> Laws restricting freedom of expression to protect national security go by several names, such as treason or sedition laws, State secrets laws, anti-terrorism laws and others. For all of these, "extreme care" must be taken to ensure that they are written and enforced in a manner, which is compatible with the three-part test[58] for restrictions.

[58] According to this text, the three-part test requires that any restriction follow the principle of legality, the principle of legitimacy (follow an objective expressed in the Civil and Political Rights Covenant) and the principle of necessity and proportionality (UNESCO 2021, 71).

> To ensure this, careful definition of "national security" and clarity in the laws is crucial. Where national security is left as an amorphous concept, there is a high risk it will be abused:
> "The concept is broadly defined and is thus vulnerable to manipulation by the State as a means of justifying actions that target vulnerable groups such as human rights defenders, journalists or activists. It also acts to warrant often unnecessary secrecy around investigations or law enforcement activities, undermining the principles of transparency and accountability" (UNESCO 2021, 65).

Moreover, this information cannot remain indefinitely or eternally in the dark because even war has rules and the decision-makers in this regard must be held accountable for them. Public authorities and officers of public forces must demonstrate that they served the best interests of the population, respecting human rights and making good use of the resources made available to them. This is what accountability is all about. Consequently, the recommendation of the OAS panel of experts is that defense and operational plans can only be kept secret as long as they are of operational use and should therefore be disclosed when they are no longer useful and the risk of them being known by enemy forces ceases[59].

European Commission Regulation 1049/2001 governing public access to European Parliament, Council and Commission documents (in force since 2001) is a starting point towards a general culture of transparency in the region. Until then, secrecy and hermeticism prevailed in the region. In fact, there has been a substantial change in this objective:

> The general rule applicable in the administrative practice of the [European] institutions could be summarized as follows: everything was secret, except for what was expressly decided to be made public and, unless the document had been classified as secret, each institution seemed to be free to determine through its regulations, or other rules of lower rank, which documents were to be considered confidential and which were not (Rams Ramos 2008, 75).

According to Rams Ramos (2008), the first European Community rules on access to information (Regulation 354/1983 and Decision 359/1983/ECSC on atomic and coal and steel information, respectively) provided for openness only after thirty years had elapsed since the production of documents, and provided they were not on the list of absolute exceptions that were highly reductive of the *right to know*.

But Regulation 1049/2001 contains a scope much more friendly to openness and transparency, compared to previous rules on parliamentary

[59] Organization of American States 2020, article 34 (1) (a).

documents, notwithstanding providing for a rather sophisticated regime of exceptions. Article 4 of this regulation describes three categories of exceptions, the first and strongest of which relates to the absolute refusal of access. This is precisely the one that deals with public security, defense and military matters, international relations and the financial, monetary or economic policy of the European Community or its members. This category also includes documents relating to the privacy and integrity of individuals, i.e. the personal data protection regime.

The second category of exception in Regulation 1049/2001 is not absolute, so the custodian of the requested information must necessarily apply a survey to determine whether the public interest in disclosing the content outweighs (or not) the interest of maintaining the confidentiality. This category inludes: the commercial interests of a physical or legal person, including intellectual property; legal proceedings and legal advice; and, the purpose of inspection, investigation and audit activities. Regarding the last two types of documents, it is clear that exposing the progress of an investigation may harm the public interest in punishing wrongdoing (inherent in the state's obligation to guarantee all human rights) and prevent impunity. Therefore, depending on each specific case, the institutions under this Regulation must analyze and reasonably explain whether it is more convenient to the public interest to disclose the required data or not.

As for administrative and criminal investigations, in principle, confidentiality applies to the early stages of an investigation, but its results must be disclosed to the public, in most cases, when these have been consolidated, since it is necessary for society to know that those acts that affect them are being effectively prosecuted by the state. Furthermore, in certain regimes, such as Ecuador's, in any case involving human rights violations, state entities are absolutely forbidden to refuse to hand over information[60], and the Ombudsman is empowered to know any confidential information (even in preliminary investigations of crimes), as well as to monitor due process[61]. The same occurs in the Mexican legislation, which establishes that information related to serious human rights violations or crimes against humanity cannot be classified as confidential[62]. The Argentine transparency law also concludes the catalog of exceptions by establishing that in cases of serious human rights violations, genocide, war

---

[60] Ecuador. Constituent Assembly 2008, Article 18 (2).

[61] Ecuador. Constituent Assembly 2008, Article 215 (4).

[62] Mexico. Chamber of Deputies of the H. Congress of the Nation 2016, Article 8.

crimes or crimes against humanity, none of the exceptions listed[63] are applicable. A regrettable tradition of secrecy supported by the law, regarding the activities of the police and military, contributed to maintaining state crimes unpunished. This led the IACrtHR to adopt a firm position on the unenforceability of the reservation in cases of serious human rights violations. This can be seen in the case of Myrna Mack Chang v. Guatemala, that expressly ruled out public-interest justifications to avoid complying with providing investigative information in such cases:

> (...) the Inter-American Court established that the Ministry of National Defense had refused to provide some documents related to the functioning and structure of the Presidential General Staff, necessary to advance the investigation of an extrajudicial execution. The Public Prosecutor's Office and the judges of the Nation had repeatedly requested this information, but the Ministry of National Defense refused to provide it, invoking the State secrecy regulated by Article 30 of the Guatemalan Constitution. According to the Inter-American Court, "in cases of human rights violations, State authorities may not rely on mechanisms such as State secrecy or confidentiality of information, or on reasons of public interest or national security, to fail to provide the information requested by the judicial or administrative authorities in charge of the pending investigation or proceedings" (Special Rapporteur for the Freedom of Expression 2012, 22).

The OAS recommendation (2020) also extends to other types of state actions to prevent impunity and raise the level of compliance of public officials in the administration of *public resources*. The term does not only include public moneys, but all kinds of assets and wealth, and sources of such, therefore requiring full transparency in public procurement, large-scale projects, social services provisions, and so on. To this end, it is also recommended that information be provided in the case of investigation of acts of corruption. In this regard, corruption is understood as a structural flaw in the political system of a country that has a pernicious effect on public life, but also on private life at many levels. Public decisions *behind closed doors* encourage corrupt practices. As Solimano (2008, 76-77) explains:

> The role of information and transparency is key to control corruption. Today, information on practices involving state property and assets is not known, or if there are no free and independent press conditions, corruption can flourish without major problems, since these practices will surely not be known or see the light of day, which shows the importance of the press and the media.

---

[63] Argentina. Senate and Chamber of Deputies 2016, Article 8. Note that this norm requires that the violations under investigation be qualified as "serious", as opposed to the Ecuadorian law that does not bear such elemento to apply for full disclosure.

Following Solimano, there is, in effect, a relationship between democracy and transparency, so that the greater the transparency, the less corruption will be perceived.

Notwithstanding the reservation or legal classification, those directly involved in a given case (victims and defendants) are not the *general public* and are always entitled to know the status of such investigations, because everyone has the right to understand the charges against him or her in order to be able to defend him or herself. Article 9.2 of the International Covenant on Civil and Political Rights provides that every person shall be promptly informed of the charges against him. In the Ecuadorian Constitution, the right of access of the person under investigation extends not only to criminal investigations, but to all areas, including the administrative ones (take for instance, administrative or tax audits), and access to the complete file is guaranteed to the person under investigation and their attorney[64]. In this case, such person will have access to the information as the owner of personal data that the state is holding on him or herself or their assets, as they make up the investigation.

Returning to the need for weighing in conflicting cases, more than two decades ago it was already established the need to demonstrate objectively and explicitly that the interest of confidentiality outweighs the interest of disclosure. Otherwise, even if the information is generally confidential, it must be disclosed to the citizens requesting it. The third paragraph of Article 4 of Regulation 1049/2001 refers to the internal activities of the Community institutions subject to it, prior to the taking of a decision, as well as to opinions in the context of deliberations or consultations. According to Rams Ramos (2008), in the latter group of exceptions, a *double test* must be applied:

> To the weighing judgment between the overriding public interest in disclosure and the harm that could result from the disclosure of the requested documents, an element of degree is added, since these exceptions may only be applied if such harm is of a serious nature ("if its disclosure would seriously undermine the decision-making process"), as opposed to the simple harm that must be assessed in the weighing prescribed in the second paragraph of Article 4 (...) (Rams Ramos 2008, 107).

This author argues that the obligation to assess has been ratified in the European context through the cases heard by the Court of Justice of the European Community, namely World Wide Fund for Nature v.

---

[64] Ecuador. Constituent Assembly 2008, article 76 (7).

Commission, Carvel and Guardian Newspapers v. Commission, Svenska Journalistförbundet v. Council and, Heidi Hautala v. Council[65]. In all these cases it was established that the custodians of the information (European institutions, commission or council) have the obligation to weigh[66], to give reasons for the refusal on the basis of such weighting, and to release the section of the information that is considered public under European law, even if there is a legitimate interest in reserving the remaining information.

With respect to the harm assessment in the balancing test, OAS establishes three criteria that allow for the refusal to provide information, because it is the duty of the custodian or holder of the information to provide a reasoned justification for the refusal. Accordingly, alleged harm must be founded on these grounds (Organization of American States 2020, 54-55):

- Real harm: the information requested represents a real risk to the public interest; hypothetical harm cannot be used as a justification for reservation.
- Demonstrable harm: the harm to the public interest would be greater if the requested information were disclosed than if access to it were restricted.
- Identifiable harm: the release of the information would seriously affect the parties involved in the facts described above.

By delimiting what will be understood as *harm* to a legal asset identified and provided for in the law, opposable to the interest in disclosure, the possibilities for the discretionary exercise of the classification of information are minimized. Therefore, greater guarantees are offered to the right of access to public information in favor of individuals. This also helps state officials to play a role in protecting information and to defend themselves in the event of a challenge. Following Claude Reyes v. Chile (2006), it is required that the balancing test verifies the inexistence of an alternative means less harmful to the right of access to information; that is to say, that a proportionality test is applied at the same time. From the foregoing, we have that it is up to the state body to prove that the information cannot be provided, instead of the petitioner proving that it deserves to be provided.

---

[65] Rams Ramos 2008, 91.

[66] Consistent with this premise is the decision in the case of Maurizio Turco and the Government of Sweden v. European Commission, which favorably heard an appeal in which, among other things, the court of first instance required the petitioner to demonstrate a public interest override with respect to the minimum standards for the reception of applicants for asylum in Member States (Sweden and Turco v Council 2008).

Mexico clearly defines it in its transparency law: the burden of proof to justify any denial of access shall correspond to the state regulated entities[67]. Under the harm test, the custodian of reserved information must demonstrate that the elements of the normative hypothesis that prevent access to the information are met. Therefore, it is not enough that the information is related to one of the criteria of confidentiality established by law (this is only the first step), but, as explained by Mendel (2008, 38), whoever intends to prevent the release of information must prove a legitimate purpose. There is a nuance of great relevance to the rule of proof, which states that the harm outbalance evidence does not intend to demonstrate the relationship of the information with any of the categories of exception, but to make it clear that the disclosure would imply the violation of an interest equally protected by law:

> As to the object of the evidence... the aim is not to prove the factual situation, but mainly the "crisis" -in the fortunate expression of Gonzaini- of the threatened or affected constitutional right. From this it follows that the parties in constitutional proceedings must attend, not to a particular interest in the evidence but to one of a general nature, to identify the norms that are contrary to the supremacy of the constitutional ones, or to identify whether a public or private act or omission is a violation of constitutional rights... (Porras Velasco 2011, 50)

And in view of the fact that these processes are guided by the *pro homine* principle, as Porras Velasco (2011) points out, in any case of doubt (that is not solved through the necessity and proportionality test), the decision must always be taken in favor of the protection and prevalence of the fundamental right of access.

So, we have that for certain projects of great public relevance, access by the people must be ensured even after a certain period of time, so that they can exercise social control over state decisions. And in other cases, even certain information that by definition would be private, must and can be known by all. But certain private information, even if relevant to the public, must be kept confidential as the private interest outweighs the public one. The difference can be graphed as follows: the "Manhattan Project", although composed of highly sensitive and therefore classified information, should have been opened to the public at some point in history so that the American people –and the world– were able to know and assess what the state did in the name of the people and with public resources, to end the Second World War. By contrast, the "Chicago Project" that developed Windows 95, though

[67] Mexico. Chamber of Deputies of the H. Congress of the Nation 2016, Article 103.

it transformed the lives of an entire generation and contributed set humanity on a different course about communication and data, has no business opening its most cherished secrets to the world because that information has not belonged to the people at any time, even if it has affected as all.

State Economic Information

The subject of state economic information is particularly interesting and is not covered in the Latin American legislations under study, and even the Inter-American Law Model only admits its exclusion when the state's capacity to manage an economic emergency is compromised[68]. On the contrary, the United Kingdom's Freedom of Information Act excludes from public access those data that cause harm to the public:

> (a) the economic interests of the United Kingdom or of any part of the United Kingdom, or
> (b) the financial interests of any administration in the United Kingdom [meaning: the government of the United Kingdom, the Scottish Administration and the Executive Committee of the Northern Ireland Assembly].

The breadth of this prohibition certainly presents difficulties when it comes to its application, since the financial and economic interests of a public administration are as vast as the activities it carries out. Here, the rules of weighing and proof of damage, which materializes in article 17 (3) of the same regulation, will become relevant, demanding that the public authority states the reasons for refusal on the following grounds:

> (a) that, in all the circumstances of the case, the public interest in maintaining the exclusion of the duty to confirm or deny outweighs the public interest in disclosing whether the authority holds the information, or
> (b) that, in all the circumstances of the case, the public interest in maintaining the exemption outweighs the public interest in disclosing the information.

However, we see that also at the level of the European Parliament, information related to monetary, financial and economic policy is excluded from the public[69].

On its part, Mexico excludes from public disclosure information that could jeopardize the *effectiveness* of the country's monetary, exchange rate

---

[68] Organization of American States 2020, Article 33 (1) (f).
[69] European Parliament and Coucil 2001, article 4 (1) (a)

and financial system policy measures[70]. Meaning that not all information of a state-economic nature is excluded, but only when its disclosure could compromise the economic security of the nation.

Procedure for Classifying Information

It is crucial for the protection of the right to information that the steps to classify data as confidential are public and established in the law, and that the rules for the treatment of such data during the time it is kept secret, as well as for its declassification, are set forth in advance. In addition, the public must know what confidential information is held by public institutions through indexes that show the period of such confidentiality and the person responsible for maintaining it and releasing it at the end of that period. The non-compliance with the legal procedure of classification of information results in the automatic publication of the information in certain legislations, such as the Ecuadorian, which determines the obligatory nature of this procedure[71]. This is not the case in the United Kingdom, where the law establishes the categorization of reserved information, but it is a public policy which outlines the procedure to categorize it as official, secret and top secret, without explicitly defining that the categorization is mandatory and prior, or the consequences of non-compliance. In fact, the Official Secrets Act 1989 makes Crown servants and contractors who handle such information liable for any unauthorized disclosure.

Returning to the classification procedure, OAS (2020, 58-62) recommends establishing minimum rules for classification to proceed:

1. The classification must precede the request for access and be based on the public interest test of the reserve.
2. The classification of a document may be partial.
3. The norm must establish a maximum period during which the information may remain out of public access: the OAS recommends five years, extendable to five additional years, but always prohibiting indefinite confidentiality.
4. Establish an index register of classified information that will always be public.
5. To appoint a guarantor body to verify compliance with the classification and declassification procedure.

---

[70] Mexico. Chamber of Deputies of the H. Congress of the Nation 2016, Article 100, XI.

[71] Ecuador. National Assembly 2023, article 17.

The initial term of five years for the classification of information on such sensitive issues as national defense plans or criminal investigations deserves a separate comment, as it may be contrary to the spirit of these rules and state objectives; even contrary to the common good. It is advisable to apply time limits appropriate to the type of information to be classified, taking into account the reasons for its confidentiality. In the case of Mexico, the period of confidentiality and extension recommended by the OAS is accepted, but not in the case of Ecuador, where the period of confidentiality is ten years, which may be extended to fifteen.

Contrary to the recommendations of the OAS, in the Mexican case[72] it is established that the classification of information will be carried out at the moment a request for access is received, which makes the system prone to establish arbitrary reservations that are not compatible with the public interest and the security and sovereignty of the state.

A specific feature that deserves special consideration is the gradation foreseen in the UK's Government Security Classifications Policy (2023) that correlates security measures with mitigation measures in case of unwanted exposure:

> OFFICIAL Definition: The majority of information that is created, processed, sent or received in the public sector and by partner organisations, which could cause no more than moderate damage if compromised and must be defended against a broad range of threat actors with differing capabilities using nuanced protective controls.
> (...)
> SECRET Definition: Very sensitive information that requires enhanced protective controls, including the use of secure networks on secured dedicated physical infrastructure and appropriately defined and implemented boundary security controls, suitable to defend against highly capable and determined threat actors, whereby a compromise could threaten life (an individual or group), seriously damage the UK's security and/or international relations, its financial security/stability or impede its ability to investigate serious and organised crime.
> (...)
> TOP SECRET Definition: Exceptionally sensitive information assets that directly support or inform the national security of the UK or its allies AND require an extremely high assurance of protection from all threats with the use of secure networks on highly secured dedicated physical infrastructure, and robustly defined and implemented boundary security controls.

[72] Mexico. Chamber of Deputies of the H. Congress of the Nation 2016, Article 98 (I).

Beyond the level of protection of certain sensitive and transcendental information for the safeguarding of high interests of the population, the confidentiality of information cannot be opposed to the prerogative of society *to know* in such a way that the activities of the authorities and state entities, the resources they manage and the decisions they make, remain concealed. Therefore, although the protection of this type of information is recognized in the law, the decisions on its confidentiality and dissemination in specific cases deserve to be carefully studied and oriented towards the broadest exercise of the rights of all interested parties. In other words, it is not only the motivation that drives the petitioner that is at stake, but also the general welfare.

Obligations of the State

In terms of public law, access to information consists of formal and material components that must be fulfilled altogether. The duty of the state to guarantee human rights is complex, given the cross-cutting nature of other rights within the same hierarchical framework, along with public interest considerations, including, but not limited to, national security, public health, non-discrimination and other significant challenges. Fundamental rights, in order to generate obligations on the state, are recognized as such by some legal act[73], the most common and vigorous of which is constitutional recognition. The ratification of international instruments recognizing rights is also a means by which the state binds itself to the citizenry and to the international community, in accordance with the terms of the recognized right, provided that it does so following the procedure defined in national legislation for such instruments to become part of the state's binding normative block. Thus, both the formal duties and the fulfillment of the core of the right itself are necessary for the state, in the person of whoever holds public power at a given time, to meet its juridical responsibility and perform the tasks deriving from each right.

Fundamental freedoms are considered indispensable to guarantee the life, dignity and survival of the individual; they generally imply a duty to *refrain from* or prohibit arbitrary intervention by the state. Clear examples are the prohibition of torture, cruel, inhuman or degrading treatment, arbitrary detention or enforced disappearances. In contrast, there are rights that mainly require *actions* on the part of the states for their fulfillment; these are called by the doctrine as *beneficial rights*. An example of these are economic, social and cultural rights. One of their main peculiarities is their progressive nature: governments must assume ever greater obligations with respect to their effective guarantee. This means that, when a right is recognized (either by ratification of or accession to an international

[73] It should be made clear that rights deriving from human dignity do not require legal positivization to be exercised. On the contrary, national or supranational legal instruments merely recognize, but do not constitute, the right that has always existed because they correspond to the human condition. However, in order to be enforceable, it is generally necessary to define their content and order the state to act accordingly, without disregarding the principle of progressiveness and the dynamism inherent to these rights.

instrument, or in domestic constitutional or legal norms), a baseline is generated. The state must demonstrate that, from that starting point, it has invested efforts (such as money, personnel, planning and time) to achieve progress in terms of the level of enjoyment of that right. Furthermore, the state is prohibited from applying regressive measures, i.e., measures that imply going backwards in the progress achieved. By way of example, a state that recognizes school breakfast as a right of children cannot remove this benefit years later, even if its fiscal resources are less healthy than before.

However, this doctrinal and historical classification of state obligations disappears in practice when it becomes clear that rights, regardless of their structural origin, require both action and abstention by the state. Even negative obligations, by definition, imply a duty to protect beyond mere refraining. For example, the duty to protect in relation to the right to life goes beyond just holding back from disposing of an individual's life: it also requires the state's duty to enact legislation prohibiting third parties from interfering with this right and to sanction the actions of third parties against a person's life. Thus, the state is also responsible for establishing an organized structure to investigate and punish any unlawful interference with the right to life. In certain cases, the state is liable for damages caused to individual and collective rights by the unlawful conduct of its officials in accordance with the doctrine of direct and strict state liability. In other cases, the state may be held liable even for events beyond its will or control, if certain conditions are met (take, for instance, the management of the COVID crisis or the way in which the state deals with the consequences of natural disasters), because the state is always responsible for the protection of the life and safety of its inhabitants.

Even when the right of access to public information has historically been recognized as an element of freedom of expression, therefore, a civil right, it shares several principles and characteristics with social rights, since it requires a high level of participation of authorities and state officials, a protective structure (with judicial remedies and specialized oversight bodies) and proactivity for proper compliance. Thus, it has similarities with the beneficial rights. Abramovich clearly defines the way in which social rights are complied with by the states:

> The State fulfills in part rights such as the right to health, housing or education, through regulations that extend obligations to individuals, by intervening in the market through regulation and the exercise of police power, a priori (through authorizations, authorizations, or licenses) or a posteriori (via supervision) Abramovich (2009, 14).

This is to signify that governments are required to undertake positive action in the real world to meet their international obligations regarding economic and social rights. Considering the above, the right to access public information is similar given that state authorities and officers need to process information for the public and respond to particular petitions. This cannot be done without proper resources and training of said officers, which constitute positive international obligations.

The guarantee of political and civil rights (*first generation* rights), as well as economic, social and cultural rights (or *second generation* rights) will produce in the state –and often in third parties– obligations of action and abstention. Third-generation or collective rights (development, environment, scientific progress, etc.) are also in this situation: the state is bound by the same duties, which are universal, to pave the way for the highest possible level of enjoyment of these rights. The correlation between information and the exercise of collective rights, such as the right to a healthy environment and to the protection of territories and ancestral lands, will be examined later in the corresponding chapter.

Now, Abramovich explains that the obligations to which the state is bound with respect to every fundamental right lie in *respecting*, *protecting* and *guaranteeing* each human right:

> Obligations to respect are defined by the duty of the State not to interfere, hinder or impede access to, or enjoyment of, the property that constitutes the object of the law. Protection obligations consist of preventing third parties from interfering with, obstructing or preventing access to such property. The obligation to insure involves ensuring that the right holder has access to the property when he or she cannot do so on his or her own. Promoting obligations are characterized by the duty to develop conditions for rightsholders to access the property (Abramovich 2009, 7).

This definition is equally applicable to the right to information in general and to the instrumental right of access in particular. The state is obliged to make information subject to disclosure available to the public so that whoever seeks it can find it. This obligation has two components: firstly, the dissemination of public information of general interest, which is necessary for the construction of public opinion and democratic debate. Secondly, the provision of information requested by individuals, which is not subject to the regime of legitimate exceptions, regardless of the reason for which it is sought. In both cases, the state must provide resources, personnel and internal guidelines, at least, to be considered in compliance with the obligation to *respect*.

To *protect* the right it is necessary to legislate against any obstruction or interference by third parties to the detriment of access to the information required by an individual or group. This implies ensuring compliance with the law by the private sector, which means that not only the state is subject to the obligations derived from this fundamental right, but also any organization or person that interacts directly with data produced using public resources or for public purposes. At the same time, a judicial or administrative remedy, or both, must be established to be activated in the event of non-compliance or violation of the law, both by state officials and private entities that maintain public information. In certain jurisdictions, such as Ecuador, those remedies include constitutional guarantees that allow citizens to access the courts in a priority manner, through an agile and effective judicial recourse. This ensures that citizens have an advanced legal remedy and can hold state officials and private entities accountable for failure to provide public information when there is a legal obligation to do so.

To *guarantee* the right, the state must remove the obstacles that prevent the widest possible enjoyment of this right. This is done in a positive way, that is, with actions that are verified in reality in the form of legislative measures, public policy, in the structuring of the state to benefit access, etc. Examples of guaranteeing the right are the establishment of schemes of proactive publication of information, appointing compliance officers responsible for responding to requests for access, providing authorities and public entities in charge of overseeing the action of the state in this regard, among others. The purpose will be to make access to the population effective and to ensure that the right does not remain a mere legal statement.

To *promote* the right of access to public information, the state must endorse education and training of public officials and civil society, so that the mechanisms of respect, protection and guarantee are useful for the objective pursued, which ultimately consists of empowering citizens through information. For the exercise of rights, knowledge of these is essential: both rights holders and state officials must be aware of the content, prerogatives and legitimate limitations they are equally bound by. To accomplish this, the state must foster a climate of respect through dissemination and other similar mechanisms that contribute to the prevention of rights violations. Promoting rights is a fourth state obligation.

By equipping public authorities and their teams with specialized knowledge and tools in information dissemination and openness, competent performance on the part of the state can be ensured, which directly results in increasing the rate of realization of the right. Similarly, educating the general public about their rights and the process of obtaining public information allows them to demand transparency from the government and private organizations, ensuring that they fulfill their obligation to provide requested information. Since the state is responsible for guaranteeing the correct application of rights, education becomes an essential component of its responsibilities. However, there may be a strong inclination to withhold information to avoid accountability, and the lack of adequate education in this area facilitates such illegitimate intentions. At the same time, the participation of civil society and non-governmental organizations, to defend a society respectful of human rights, is crucial to the exercise and enjoyment of human rights. In fact, there are theories that consider that social mobilization and even civil disobedience is highly effective in pushing for a more rights-guaranteeing state. Regardless of the form this mobilization takes (democracy often comes with a little disorder), adequate and timely information will feed public opinion. To that extent, information enhances social participation.

In sum, international human rights treaties require states to[74]:

1. Respect the rights provided for in international instruments;
2. Undertake the necessary legislative procedures to give effect to each right recognized therein;
3. To ensure justice in case of violation of such rights;

[74] E.g. Article 2.1 through 2.3 of the International Covenant of Civil and Political Rights: 1. Each State Party to the present Covenant undertakes to respect and to ensure to all individuals within its territory and subject to its jurisdiction the rights recognized in the present Covenant, without distinction (...) 2. Where not already provided for by existing legislative or other measures, each State Party to the present Covenant undertakes to take the necessary steps, in accordance with its constitutional processes and with the provisions of the present Covenant, to adopt such laws or other measures as may be necessary to give effect to the rights recognized in the present Covenant.
Each State Party to the present Covenant undertakes:
(a) To ensure that any person whose rights or freedoms as herein recognized are violated shall have an effective remedy, notwithstanding that the violation has been committed by persons acting in an official capacity;
(b) To ensure that any person claiming such a remedy shall have his right thereto determined by competent judicial, administrative or legislative authorities, or by any other competent authority provided for by the legal system of the State, and to develop the possibilities of judicial remedy;
(c) To ensure that the competent authorities shall enforce such remedies when granted.

4. To guarantee the execution of remedies dictated by the competent authorities to repair any violation of those rights and avoid those violations from happening again.

In short, all states are obliged to respect these rights, ensuring that any arbitrary interference in the exercise or enjoyment of them are duly and timely neutralized. Moreover, in order to guarantee fundamental rights, states must adapt their internal norms, institutions, officials and, in general terms, the state structure that guides it towards the realization and enjoyment of the right, as required by the content or core of the same. These are the general characteristics of the international obligations to which states are compelled to. Each right, according to its characteristics, has a set of specific obligations that states must fulfill. In the case of access to information, the obligations are both negative (of non-interference) and positive (of enforcement), which has meant a change for states, especially because civil and political rights, which belong to the first generation of rights, have historically been understood to bear only negative compulsions.

Now, with respect to the right of access to information specifically, the first state obligation is, without a doubt, to deliver public information in due time and form, guaranteeing its usefulness for its legitimate owner: the citizens. When the information exists in the entity that has been requested and complies with the characteristics that provide it with legal protection and make it *deliverable* to the citizen, the state's duty is simply fulfilled with the delivery made in accordance with the law. Part of the guarantee of access is that the information is useful to the person requesting it, regardless of its purpose. Furthermore, the state's obligations are limited to providing the information they hold and, except where the law or deliverable commitments require it, they are not obliged to *produce* information (some cases where this duty exists are discussed below). Thus, it goes beyond the right of access to request that the state entity or authority evaluate, analyze, or perform acts on the basis of the obligation it possesses: such activities may be subject to other fundamental rights, such as the right to a good public administration. However, the activities that are implicit in the right of access is that the information be available, and for it to be available, it is essential that it be compiled, classified, ordered, systematized, filed and indexed. Although the omission of these activities cannot be resolved by citizen request, it will cause a breach by the state entity because it will not be able to comply, in time and form, with the delivery of the information. It will then be the responsibility of the person in charge of the file to sanction the culprit and organize the information in order to comply with the citizen's request. The administrative and judicial authorities may determine, based on international standards, that the information is indeed properly organized to be delivered.

Since the multiplicity of objectives that citizens may have in relation to the information they require is virtually impossible to address, common delivery rules include:

- Form of the request: the citizen may request the information from the entity that holds it. Generally, the access rules provide that, if the person has submitted a request before an entity that is not responsible for the information requested, it is the duty of such body to explain it promptly and, if possible, to direct it to the entity holding the information. Institutions must inform individuals how to submit their access requests through their websites, as a general rule, as well as to identify the officer in charge of handling such a request.
- Time: each access regulation establishes a maximum time limit within which the access request must be responded to. The deadlines range from ten to thirty days[75].
- Means: traditionally, the delivery of information was made through copies of the source that contains it, which implies an expense that is assigned to the interested party or petitioner. Nowadays, supranational norms and access laws provide solutions so that the cost of access is not so onerous as to prevent or dissuade the exercise of the right, which would constitute an obstacle to be removed according to the international obligations of the states. It is even foreseen that if the petitioner is so vulnerable that he/she cannot cover the cost of reproducing the information media, the state must cover it. However, digital media that reduce the cost of reproduction and the response time are increasingly being used. This, however, implies a new challenge: the so-called digital illiteracy may present new obstacles. Once again, it is the state that must remove barriers to the exercise of the right by ensuring that the information is delivered in such a way that it remains useful to the petitioner. Even when the information is highly technical, as is the case, for example, with environmental information, the state must simplify the information so that it can be understood by those who need to be informed. On the other side, the state is required to produce

[75] For example, the Aarhus Convention and the Escazu Agreement establish a thirty-day deadline for the delivery of environmental information, considering, it is understood, the high technical level and specificity of this type of data. This deadline does not apply if the domestic legislation of the state provides for a shorter one.

information in the official languages, languages of intercultural relations, languages accessible to persons with disabilities, and other languages spoken or used in the country, so as to ensure that the information effectively fulfills its function of *informing*.

- Partial release: the notion that, when there is partially confidential or reserved information, the section that is considered public must be released to the applicant is becoming more and more generalized. Under certain circumstances in which the danger of dissemination could impede the exercise of public functions, the authorities have ensured that the right of access refers to the source or container of the information, so that the reproduction of the same would not be part of the right and it would be sufficient for the petitioner to physically access the file to review it, without the possibility of photocopying or photographing it. Nevertheless, all the regulations studied incorporate reproduction and delivery as part of the right to seek information.
- Oversight body: all legislations provide for an oversight body to supervise the application of the law and neutralize actions or omissions by public authorities contrary to the right of access. This body generally assumes functions such as the production of standards and indexes of information to be published and assumes a role of first instance in case of disputes over particular requests for access to information that have been denied by any authority.

But the state's obligations do not end there. It turns out that there are duties that require state activity directly related to the production and/or dissemination of specific information. The following are some of the cases in which the state not only must provide information but is also obliged to produce it.

Duty to Actively Produce Information

Legal experts who have studied this issue find conflicts over the state's duty to produce information. This is because the right of access seems to be limited to the state body that *allows* the citizen *to* access the source of the information held by that body. That is, the duty would focus on providing existing information or bringing it as close as possible to the citizens by the obliged public administration, with its always limited resources. But the state has a definite positive obligation regarding access to information, which is to produce it under a legal mandate or compelled by circumstances, in order to comply with its functions. One of those functions is, for example, crime investigation and justice administration. Another one, the building of statistics for decision-making in all aspects of society. Another, the counting of votes in public elections. And so on. Therefore, for the OAS Freedom of Expression Rapporteurship, the duty goes beyond passive respect:

> The State has the obligation to produce or capture the information it needs for the fulfillment of its duties, as established by international, constitutional or legal norms (Special Rapporteur on Freedom of Expression 2010, para. 35).

Therefore, it is not enough to passively allow an individual to review a file or document in which he or she expresses an interest; the state is obliged to take steps to grant access to certain data, and to do so, the data must first be produced.

Proactive Publishing

To ensure publicity, the Inter-American Law Model prepared by the OAS (2020, article 5) proposes a set of key data that must be disseminated proactively, without the need for a citizen request. The first obligation to produce information refers to basic data on the functioning, legal capacity, authority, budget and resources, and powers of public administrations. The aim is for the citizen to understand the functioning of the state and to be able to exercise rights and reasonably fulfill obligations on the basis of the information provided by the state. The details to be published by public institutions are usually included in second or third-class legal texts. Meanwhile, the UK rule delegates to each public authority the creation of a publication scheme containing the information it considers relevant to actively disseminate. To that effect, the Information Commissioner is in charge of generating a model scheme, but it is not mandatory for public authorities, which may generate their own scheme. In any case, the publication scheme must be approved by the Commissioner. The information to be contained in the scheme is described in section 19 (2A) of the Freedom of Information Act:

> A publication scheme must, in particular, include a requirement for the public authority concerned-
> (a) to publish-
> (i) any dataset held by the authority in relation to which a person makes a request for information to the authority, and
> (ii) any up-dated version held by the authority of such a dataset, unless the authority is satisfied that it is not appropriate for the dataset to be published,

> (b) where reasonably practicable, to publish any dataset the authority publishes by virtue of paragraph (a) in an electronic form which is capable of re-use (...) (Parliament of the United Kingdom, 2022).

As mentioned earlier, it is also relevant for citizens to know what information is being excluded from the public because it has been classified as confidential. Thus, the law designates the control entity to publish the indexes of reserved information proactively in the Argentinean case[76] and Mexican[77], while in the Ecuadorian case the index is published by each entity that acts as the custodian of the information of this kind. In any instance, the index of classified information must be known by all, prohibiting its classification, and this is ratified by the OAS (2020, Article 6 (A) (j) (k) (l)), which also requires that it must be disclosed when the information has been declassified.

Countries such as Argentina and Mexico, which have a federal structure, or the United Kingdom, which consists of several nations, must comply with national and local regulations, as there are obligations related to proactive publication in numerous regulatory bodies. Moreover, even in unitarist countries such as Ecuador, basic publishable information can be found in various texts, not only in the access to public information regime.

The Inter-American Law Model (OAS 2020, Article 6) also suggests imposing as a requirement the proactive publication of information that may affect a particular population:

- Gender equality, including statistics on labor inclusion, salary gap and health.
- Priority groups such as children, elderly, indigenous and afro-descendant communities and diverse gender identification.
- Subsidies in favor of certain sectors.
- Indicators on social impact.
- Standards to measure the level of human rights protection, among others.

The active publication of this type of data is intended to increase the level of accountability of public decisions that impact groups in situations of vulnerability or historically relegated ones, and to promote community participation in those decisions, mainly of those directly affected.

---

[76] Argentina. Senate and Chamber of Deputies 2016, article 24 (s).

[77] Mexico. Chamber of Deputies of the H. Congress of the Nation 2016, article 101.

Regarding the importance of publicity for citizens, the Constitutional Court of Ecuador[78] examined the legal effectiveness of a series of administrative norms changing the timing of tax complaints and audits issued by the tax administration. Those norms had not been duly published in the context of the pandemic due to COVID-19, finding that the administration did not comply with its obligations with respect to the right to legal certainty and non-retroactivity of the law, by omitting publication in the official gazette under the excuse that an unforeseeable circumstance (the pandemic) had occurred. The Court noted that the regulations of the tax administration could not be considered promulgated and, therefore, would be deprived of their legal effect on taxpayers during the period between the issuance and the publication made in accordance with the law, so that their content would be void during that period if it prejudiced the right of defense and other rights of the taxpayers[79]. This precedent ratified that publicity of administrative activity is not optional: if a norm is not published it may not be enforced.

Another specific group of information of public interest that imposes an obligation on the state to produce information relates to the environment. In accordance with Advisory Opinion OC-23/17 issued by the IACrtHR (2017), it is stated that Article 5 of the Escazú Agreement imposes an obligation on the state to produce or compile information in the environmental sphere. This obligation requires an active participation of the state, and no longer a passive role of waiting for citizens to submit petitions. It is the state's duty to inform rather than the citizen's obligation to reach out for information. Nevertheless, political participation is not only a right of the people but also a democratic responsibility. The state's failure to proactively and timely produce and disseminate information in this case could be considered an affectation of rights actionable under the Agreement.

---

[78] Andrade v. SRI 2023.

[79] In this regard, the previous version of the Inter-American Law Model provided for the ineffectiveness of public policies that had not been published proactively and in a timely manner:
Article 13 stated:
(1) Public policy documents shall be publicly accessible.
(2) No one shall suffer any harm as a result of the implementation of a public policy which has not been disclosed in accordance with paragraph (1) of this article.
The current version of the Model does not deal with the effectiveness of norms duly published prior to their application.

Information on the Level of Enjoyment and Exercise of Rights

States have a responsibility to gradually increase the scope of rights enjoyment and exercise, reduce inequality-related disparities, and persuade others of their commitment to the rights they have formally acknowledged by ratifying and upholding international human rights treaties. To ensure that the population experiences the utmost level of satisfaction, the state must generate statistical data and share it with its citizens, while also reporting it to the international organizations established by each of these instruments. This matter is especially pertinent when assessing advancements in economic, social, and cultural rights. The Inter-American Commission of Human Rights sheds light on this obligation:

> The production of duly disaggregated information, for the purpose of determining these disadvantaged or neglected sectors in the exercise of rights, from this perspective, is not only a means to guarantee the effectiveness of a public policy, but an indispensable obligation for the State to comply with its duty to provide these sectors with special and priority attention. By way of example, the disaggregation of data by sex, race or ethnicity is an essential tool for shedding light on problems of inequality
> (...)
> The IACHR recalled that, "the Committee on Economic, Social and Cultural Rights has specified that it is a State obligation to produce databases from which it is possible to validate indicators and, in general, access to many of the guarantees covered by each social right". (Special Rapporteur for the Freedom of Expression 2012, 13).

The information makes it possible to identify the regression or progress of these rights, and without objective data that defines a baseline it will not be possible to measure the achievement of goals:

> (...) one of the parameters for identifying the essential content of a social right is [the] degree of protection already achieved by a given legal system. The fundamental point of this question is given by the impossibility of knowing the exact content of the state obligation without previously knowing the state of enjoyment of a social right... the Covenant [Economic, Social and Cultural Rights] imposes on the States the obligation to survey and produce information (Abramovich & Curtis, cited by Silva Portero 2007, 53-54).

Risk Management

In the face of natural or anthropogenic risks, the Constitution of Ecuador establishes the mandate to generate, democratize access to and disseminate sufficient and timely information to adequately manage risk (Article 389). This highlights the fact that in different areas of public affairs there may be deeper proactive publication obligations than those provided for in the general regime.

The importance of information in making timely decisions about the life, health and safety of individuals has also been analyzed by the ECrtHR. In Guerra et al. v. Italy, a case involving a group of families suing the Italian state for failing to provide adequate and timely information about the risks to their health posed by the proximity of a pesticide factory to their homes, a compelling need to produce information and disseminate it to stakeholders in a timely manner was recognized, as this would have guaranteed other fundamental rights, namely, the right to private and family life:

> Although the purpose of Article 8 [of the European Convention on Human Rights] is essentially to protect the individual from arbitrary interference by the authorities, it is not limited exclusively to the State's refraining from such interference: in addition to this abstention, there must be inherent obligations that give effect to respect for private and family life (Mendel, 2003).

Being the state responsible for guaranteeing not only access to public information but also the inviolability of life, health and the environment, the free development of the individual, among other basic rights of human dignity, the state must guarantee people a framework in which their private life is inviolable. So, the state has an obligation to produce and disseminate information to avoid serious harm to the life, property or other interests of individuals. Acting with secrecy in such cases can provoke a massive violation of human rights and put citizens or human coexistence at serious risk. This link between timely and quality information and the protection of life was experienced by all of humanity at once during the COVID-19 pandemic. The issue was urgently addressed by the UN, the Inter-American Commission of Human Rights and the Council of Europe, which called for the respect of human rights in the context of the pandemic, and particularly to maintain good information management, guaranteeing freedom of expression and the rights it entails. For example, the Inter-American Commission demanded that states parties guarantee human rights under special considerations to address the effects of the 2020 social, economic and health crisis, emphasizing the needs of vulnerable groups, human rights defenders, traditionally excluded groups, with approaches based on age and gender. It also urged states to intervene in the health and pharmaceutical market to make medicine and technology available to the population[80]. At the same time, the Commission expressed its concern about public information, stressing the need to prioritize and guarantee access to it. The Commission also stressed the importance of safeguarding investigators involved in public oversight activities related to the pandemic, protecting them from any unauthorized interference, whether in civil or criminal investigations. Therefore, it can be inferred that maintaining proper transmission of information becomes crucial during emergencies and unforeseen events. The recommendation implies that even if states are not directly responsible for a particular harm, they have a duty to minimize its impact by ensuring compliance, enforcement and safeguarding of human rights. This confirms the transversality and instrumentality of the right of access to public information that the Commission and the Court in the Americas have been consistently developing in recent decades. The Commission recommended to states to:

> Ensure the right to access public information in the framework of the emergency caused by COVID-19, and not set general limits based on reasons of security or public order. The bodies and officials that guarantee this right should give priority to requests for access to information related to the public health emergency, and also proactively report in detail on the impact of the pandemic and on emergency spending, and do so in an open format accessible to all vulnerable groups, in accordance with best practices internationally. If deadlines for requests for information on matters not linked to the pandemic have to be extended, governments should explain the denial, set a time period in which the obligation will be met, and allow for appeals against such decisions. (Inter-American Commission of Human Rights 2020, para. 32).

The Obligation to Investigate Violations of Rights

The right to the truth, as coined by various legislations, including Argentina's, after its painful history of massive human rights violations, entails the obligation to make known to the victims and to society the facts and circumstances related to such violations, as well as to bring the perpetrators to justice, or at least identify them, when they are already deceased. It is widely known that the disappearances caused by the de facto governments in Argentina and Chile (and by certain governments in Ecuador and other countries as well), have disrupted the lives of a large number of individuals and families, in addition to affecting at least three

[80] Inter-American Commission of Human Rights 2020, 4.

generations of people, who have demanded to know in depth the facts of which they have been direct or indirect victims, beyond the possibility of criminal prosecution of those facts.

> (...) the State has the obligation to produce, recover, reconstruct or capture the information it needs to fulfill its duties, as established by international, constitutional or legal norms. In this sense, for example, if information that it should have custody of was destroyed or illegally removed, and it was necessary to clarify human rights violations, the State must make every effort in good faith to recover or reconstruct such information, in the terms already described (Special Rapporteur for the Freedom of Expression 2012, 45).

The IACrtHR has developed the concept of the "right to the truth", which consists of the following:

> (...) the right to the truth is subsumed in the right of the victim or his relatives to obtain clarification of the events that violated human rights and the corresponding responsibilities of the competent organs of the State, through the investigation and prosecution established in Articles 8 and 25 of the Convention.
> (...) it is not enough for individuals simply to have access to information already held by the State. The State must also ensure that information on past human rights violations is readily available, including the collection, ordering, preservation and dissemination of this information (Mendel 2008, 19).

Ecuador, as well as other countries in the region and the world, established a Truth Commission to investigate violations of fundamental freedoms that occurred between 1984 and 2008. The Commission worked on these investigations (countless cases) for four years, at the end of which it submitted the results to the Attorney General's Office. The Truth Commissions have been supported by the Inter-American Commission, which recognizes the need to establish autonomous and highly ethical investigative bodies when it comes to clarifying rights violations and crimes against humanity perpetrated by state agents or with their participation or acquiescence:

> Truth commissions are one of the most commonly used mechanisms in comparative perspective by countries confronting a past of massive human rights violations. According to the International Center for Transitional Justice (ICTJ), "truth commissions" are non-judicial, independent panels of inquiry generally established to establish the facts and context of past mass violations of human rights or international humanitarian law (ICTJ definition, available at http://www.ictj.org). Among the countries that have

> used these mechanisms to shed light on crimes committed in their past are Argentina, Haiti, Guatemala, South Africa, Peru, East Timor, Ghana and Sierra Leone (Special Rapporteur for the Freedom of Expression 2012, 33).

The ethical character of its members will always be a subjective matter and the establishment of this type of ad-hoc commissions seems more compatible with a loss or serious absence of institutionality in a country. Ensuring the rule of law and strengthening the countries' own entities is in line with the self-determination of peoples. However, in the face of massive, systematic and/or structural violations of human rights, the reestablishment of institutions may require time and resources that are not immediately available, as occurs after a war, a coup d'état or at the return to democracy. The contribution of these commissions to the clarification of facts that otherwise would have taken an enormous amount of time to investigate, if they had been investigated at all, is undeniable. However, abusing this mechanism is extremely dangerous; it should not be taken to such an extent that they overrule the administration of justice system. To *oversee the overseers* is recommendable in any case.

In a paradigmatic IACrtHR case on the protection of women's lives in situations of extreme violence ("Campo Algodonero"), it became clear that, eight years after the opening of investigations into the disappearance, rape and death of three women (two of them minors) found with signs of torture in a cotton field in the city of Juarez, the Mexican Public Prosecutor's Office had still not passed the preliminary phase, repeating examinations and causing the loss of transcendental evidentiary elements. Therefore, the Court found the Mexican state guilty of having failed to comply with its duty to investigate –and thus its duty to guarantee– the rights to life, personal integrity and personal liberty, enshrined in the American Convention and the Convention of Belém do Pará on women's protection against violence. The judgment includes the words of the Special Rapporteur on Judicial Independence regarding the failure of the State to investigate these events:

> According to the UN Rapporteur on Judicial Independence, after a visit to Ciudad Juarez in 2001, '[h]e was struck by the absolute inefficiency, incompetence, indifference, insensitivity and negligence of the police who had conducted the inquiries until then' (Gonzalez and Others (Cotton Field) v. Mexico 2009, 44).

This is one of the many cases that shows that the state has an active duty to produce information and collect data to clarify the facts that have caused harm to the rights of individuals. This duty does not correspond only to the most serious acts of human rights violations, since it stems from the state's obligation to guarantee the life and integrity of all, but it takes on greater relevance when it comes to investigating, punishing and preventing this type of acts exacerbated in violence and profoundly harmful at the social level.

ENVIRONMENTAL INFORMATION, COLLECTIVE RIGHTS AND ACCESS TO JUSTICE

The right of access to public information was traditionally associated with journalistic work and its influence in shaping public opinion. Thus, the jurisprudence of supranational courts has recognized that the *search* for information is part of freedom of expression, as recognized in the American Convention on Human Rights, since without investigation there would be no journalism. In fact, in certain cases of the ECrtHR it seems that only journalists have the right to request information. But the right does not remain static and as society advocates for a much more participatory, democratic and transparent regime[81], we have come to experience that every person and group should be guaranteed access to public information regardless of whether it pursues a social purpose (such as informing through the media) or just a personal one. Once again, information is an *asset* whose ownership corresponds to individuals, and as is elementary to the right to property, it is guaranteed that the legitimate owners may use the objects of their possession in the way they prefer, as long as they respect the rights of others. Just as the owner of a house can do with it as he sees fit, as long as he does not infringe the law, the owner of information (every citizen) can reach out for it and use it as long as he does not disturb the right to honor of others, the legitimate secrets of private entities or collective security.

Like the right to inform and be informed, the right of access to public information has two dimensions: an individual one, which is the power of a citizen to request information and have it delivered upon verifying that it constitutes public information; and a collective one, as a form of containment of the state apparatus and control of the actions of its

[81] According to Ackerman (2008, 23) "(...) in many contexts the most effective type of civil society for government oversight would correspond to an irreverent, distrustful, politicized and even disorganized or decentralized civil society (...) Those who resisted authority and raised their voices to defend their rights are the ones truly responsible for democratization and government improvement in the country, unlike those who trusted in the infallibility of their leaders".

representatives[82]. Since access to information is the first step for social control, its exercise does not only benefit the person interested in obtaining it, but also achieves a collective benefit by initiating a process of accountability or socialization and public decision making that may lead to the activation of channels of dialogue, complaint and demand by the citizenry. In the defense of fundamental rights, both dimensions converge because, on the basis of the information obtained –whether it has been actively disseminated by the state or requested by the citizenry– judicial or administrative defensive or offensive actions will be brought if a violation of rights is detected.

Such defensive or offensive actions will have a result that will translate into progress or an undesirable setback in terms of fundamental rights that will have repercussions for the entire population. The collective dimension of the right to information has been recognized by the ECrtHR, which has understood the social need to maintain "watchdogs" to monitor the actions of the state and their consonance with the rights recognized in the human rights charters[83].

The relationship between information and advocacy becomes clear when it comes to the environment and the collective rights of tribal and indigenous communities. The exercise of collective rights recognized for certain ethnic groups often requires timely, verified and quality information. Thus, the right of access to public information becomes, more than ever, instrumental, as it is configured as a right-means[84] to achieve the realization

---

[82] The IACrtHR recognizes the two dimensions of the right to information in several of its rulings, as follows: (...) it is necessary that freedom of expression is a means for the exchange of ideas and information among people; it includes their right to try to communicate their points of view to others, but it also implies the right of everyone to know opinions, stories and news provided by others. For the common citizen, the knowledge of the opinion of others or of the information available to others is as important as the right to disseminate one's own (...)
This Court has affirmed that both dimensions are equally important and must be fully guaranteed simultaneously in order to give full effect to the right to freedom of expression in the terms provided by Article 13 of the Convention (Gómez Gallardo 2006).

[83] Among others, in Magyar Helsinki Bizottság v. Hungary (2016), in which it was verified that the need to access allegedly private information of public defenders was of a better category than the need to protect their reputation.

[84] For Ackerman (2008, 19), transparency can only be considered as a means in the *democratic rule of law*, since its end will always be participation and social justice. Thus, information plays an empowering role more than anything else. According to the author: "*It would be a mistake to deify these practices* [transparency and accountability] *as if they were ends in themselves*".

of other rights-purposes, such as participation in the adoption of public decisions on ancestral lands. In this way, the exercise of the collective rights recognized exclusively to indigenous peoples and other ethnic groups is strengthened when they freely and voluntarily, and sufficiently informed, participate in the public debate with voice and vote, without outside interference. Moreover, part of the right to participation implies a genuine debate in which manipulation of the opinion of the community participating in the decision-making process is proscribed. In this way, the involvement of the entire population is sought, and not only of local political leaders, without ignoring their community leadership, but providing a voice to all actors and representation to all groups. In such cases, the relationship between information and the defense of territories, as well as self-determination, can be clearly observed. These premises pose a serious challenge for states, civil society and the communities themselves.

Thus, the production of information, in addition to being a state duty, is presented as a necessity for both the population and the authorities in order to guarantee collective rights, which may even include the distribution of income from activities that have a significant environmental impact on their territories. But, in addition, the state must allocate sufficient resources for the control and supervision of these activities as well as for environmental remediation and environmental and social compensation to the most directly affected communities. Therefore, the information must reveal, in a reliable manner, who will participate in the decision, who will control the plans as they are implemented, and who will be compensated for enduring the execution of large-scale projects. While state recognition of an ancestral people is not indispensable for the exercise of their collective rights, the lack of information on their ethnic composition and historical occupation of the territory prevents distinguishing the true rights holders from those who camouflage themselves to divert and often co-opt the will and decision-making capacity of such groups, perverting their social participation. This is a highly relevant issue because, as with the right to information –which does not protect erroneous messages, ill-intentioned propaganda, rumors and other forms of disinformation– the right to participation of indigenous communities is not available to anyone who seeks to *abuse* it and adopt a position of power alien to the collective good of the community.

Concomitantly, the guarantee of individual or collective rights requires access to complete information to be able to defend, before the courts if necessary, the rights that are violated by the state, first of all, and to a lesser extent and under specific circumstances, by private actors such as corporations and organizations. Not only are collective rights of common interest, but the defense of any of the fundamental rights will result in the improvement of the level of enjoyment and exercise of rights for all people. Therefore, it is undoubtful that, by defending a fundamental right, the collective will benefit because an advance in this sense is a greater guarantee for the society in general, even beyond state borders. Thus, it is important to relate the activation of judicial guarantees with access to information because in human rights litigation, the availability of high-quality information, makes a battle with equality of arms become plausible. Proof of facts and damages is virtually impossible without timely, sufficient and adequate information, and, in many cases, that information is public and state-produced, so it cannot be denied... in theory. This chapter addresses these important topics to demonstrate that without information, the defense of rights is deficient.

Access to Environmental Information

The Aarhus Convention, applicable in the European region, and the Escazu Agreement, applicable in the Americas, are cornerstones for facilitating access to environmental information and promoting community involvement in decision-making processes. However, prior to their implementation, the connection between the effective protection of the environment and the need for accurate and adequate information, delivered in a timely manner, to enable well-informed decisions in the context of large-scale projects, extractive activities, emerging technologies, genetic modification, etc., had already been anticipated. Since the establishment of the United Nations, there have been advancements in the development of rights pertaining to the safeguarding of health and the environment[85]. In 1966, the UN General Assembly adopted, on the same date, the International Covenant on Civil and Political Rights and the International Covenant on Economic, Social and Cultural Rights. The latter contains the right to the enjoyment of the highest attainable standard of health, which requires states to "*improve the environment*" (Article 12 (b)). Over the decades, the right to a healthy environment has strengthened the protection of its elements and today we are witnessing the beginning of a paradigm shift from the traditional human understanding of nature and its resources as part of man's domain to an ecocentric dimension that even implies human obligations *towards* the

[85] For the study of the evolution of the recognition of rights in the international context, through treaties and conventions, the formation of the General Assembly of the United Nations and its predecessor, the Society of Nations, are historical milestones. However, there are several points of departure on the recognition of human rights in the planetary timeline, that are equally relevant and offer important advancements to the field.

environment, so that nature and its determined or determinable elements become a subject of protection (instead of a protected object). Several countries have recognized the legal personality of nature in the last twenty years:

- Ecuador: first country in the world to recognize specific rights to nature[86] in its highest legal norm, the national Constitution.
- Bolivia: also recognized the rights of nature in its legal framework.
- New Zealand: maintains legal norms that recognize nature's rights and two rulings have recognized rights to the Urewera forest and the Whanganui River, respectively.
- India: Through jurisprudential precedents, a judge undertook the recognition of nature as a vulnerable being in need of protection.
- Colombia: through the Constitutional Court, rights were recognized in favor of the Atrato River.
- Panama: recognizes the rights of nature to exist, persist and regenerate.
- Uganda: enacted an environmental law that includes the rights of nature.

A common denominator unites all these jurisdictions: the richness of their biodiversity and the active participation of the communities, not only as groups that protect the environment –as if it were someone else's property– but under the understanding of the symbiosis in which human beings find themselves with respect to nature, where cooperation between species is manifested as a form of survival, even if not the only one.

A striking transition arises, similar to that which occurred in the 1980s with the recognition of children's rights. That process also imposed the obligation to consider children and adolescents as *persons* entitled to the enjoyment of human rights[87], but with the need for representatives to ensure their full exercise and their best interests (a role undertaken by parents, family members, judges or other public officials). This shift in focus is also present in environmental protection and collective human health rights. It reflects a growing awareness of the interconnectedness between human well-being and the health of the planet. Derived from this recognition, the law (the Ecuadorian Constitution, for example), states any person or

[86] According to articles 71 and 72, the rights that nature must enjoy are: to its existence (similar to the human right to life), to its maintenance (similar to the human right of integrity), to the regeneration of its vital cycles and to its restoration.

[87] Until then, minors were considered objects of legal protection, but not human individuals.

organization or the Ombudsman is entitled to file claims on behalf of nature for the protection of the rights of such third-party rights holder, who is unable to enforce them in its own behalf. The mere representative, however, does not have the capacity of disposition nor can he decide to *refrain* from exercising a certain right, because such a representative has the obligation to look after the best interests of the true holder who is incapable of acting on his own behalf. Nature is, in this manner, a *being* entitled to rights.

Principle 10 of the Rio Declaration on Environment and Development[88], as well as Articles 4, 5 and 6 of the Aarhus Convention and Articles 5, 6 and 7 of the Escazú Agreement correlate information with public decision-making in which the environment is in any way affected, even in the face of potential or unconfirmed damage. These last two instruments exhibit standards of great relevance for the demand of the participation rights of the communities and that could also be attributed to nature as a rights holder (with certain nuances). According to these instruments, the state is obliged to produce, update and order (including geo-referencing) certain minimum environmental information, which must also be actively disseminated. Here is a summary of the basic requirements for the production and dissemination of environmental information in the Aarhus and Escazú instruments:

Aarhus Convention	Escazú Agreement
- Updated environmental information relevant to public functions. - In the event of imminent threat to human health or the environment, information must be disseminated with no delay for prevention or mitigation. - The type and scope of environmental information and the process to obtain it by the public.	- The text of environmental legislation, policies and international treaties. - Reports on the state of the environment. - The list of public entities with environmental legal capacities. - The list of contaminated zones and type of contamination and localization.

[88] Principle 10: Environmental issues are best handled with the participation of all concerned citizens, at the relevant level. At the national level, each individual shall have appropriate access to information concerning the environment that is held by public authorities, including information on hazardous materials and activities in their communities, and the opportunity to participate in decision-making processes. States shall facilitate and encourage public awareness and participation by making information widely available. Effective access to judicial and administrative proceedings, including redress and remedy, shall be provided.

<table>
<tr>
<td>- Publicly accessible lists, registers and files, supporting information researchers.

- Reports on the state of the environment, environmental legislation, policies and international treaties.

- Pollution inventories and reporting.

- Encourage operators of activities with significant environmental impact to inform the public, on a regular basis, of their activities, products and self-auditing schemes if applicable.

- Enable consumers to make informed environmental choices.</td>
<td>- Information on the use and preservation of natural resources and ecosystemic services.

- Academic reports on environmental research; sources on climate change.

- Procedures for the environmental impact assessment and other management resources.

- Sustainability reports for large-scale companies to reflect their social and environmental performance (not mandatory).

- Administrative sanctions.

- In the event of imminent threat to human health or the environment, information must be disseminated with no delay for prevention of damages.

- Every five years (at least), publish information on the state of the environment and natural resources, national actions for the fulfillment of environmental obligations, progress in the right to access, cooperation agreements.</td>
</tr>
</table>

Following the general line on withholding information when there may be harm to protected public or private interests, the Aarhus Convention provides for absolute (Article 4.3) and relative (Article 4.4) limitations on the release of information. In the latter case, in order to withhold the information and avoid disclosing it to the public, the state must demonstrate that the harm claimed to be caused by disclosure would outweigh the harm that would be caused by confirming its secrecy. However, the list of grounds for withholding information is limited only to the following:

> (a) The confidentiality of the proceedings of public authorities, where such confidentiality is provided for under national law;
> (b) International relations, national defense or public security;
> (c) The course of justice, the ability of a person to receive a fair trial or the ability of a public authority to conduct an enquiry of a criminal or disciplinary nature;
> (d) The confidentiality of commercial and industrial information, where such confidentiality is protected by law in order to protect a legitimate economic interest. Within this framework, information on emissions which is relevant for the protection of the environment shall be disclosed;
> (e) Intellectual property rights;
> (f) The confidentiality of personal data and/or files relating to a natural person where that person has not consented to the disclosure of the information to the public, where such confidentiality is provided for in national law;
> (g) The interests of a third party which has supplied the information requested without that party being under or capable of being put under a legal obligation to do so, and where that party does not consent to the release of the material;
> (h) The environment to which the information relates, such as the breeding sites of rare species.

The Escazú Agreement only admits four scenarios for denial of environmental information (Article 5.6):

> a) When making the information public could endanger the life, safety or health of a natural person;
> b) When making the information public would adversely affect national security, public safety or national defense;
> c) When making the information public would adversely affect the protection of the environment, including any threatened or endangered species;
> d) When making the information public would create a clear, probable and specific risk of significant harm to law enforcement, or to the prevention, investigation and prosecution of crime.

On the latter, it's important to remember that such a risk may not be hypothetic; it must be real, demonstratable an identifiable, according to the Inter-American standard.

The following lines will set out the context of some of the collective rights in which the relationship with access to information is most prominent.

Collective rights of indigenous peoples in America

Collective rights related to the ethnic character of communities have been recognized to ancestral peoples for at least the past four decades. The reality of their existence, continuity in time and place in today's nations, has been included in several international human rights instruments, with the purpose of ensuring their survival as an ethnic collective. Beyond the life and reproduction of its members, it is a matter of protecting the reproduction of the immaterial characteristics of their identity, in the space they have occupied since time immemorial. In this way, their forms of life and organization are safeguarded, but at the same time humanity is favored with the richness of diversity. Some important instruments on the protection of the collective rights of indigenous peoples and nationalities include:

- 1989: 169 International Labor Organization ("ILO") Convention.
- 1992: Rio de Janeiro Declaration on the Environment.
- 2007: United Nations Declaration on the Rights of Indigenous Peoples
- 2016: Paris Agreement (and the United Nations Framework Convention on Climate Change).
- 2018: Escazú Agreement.

The connection between land and the environment, and the cultural development and survival of ancestral indigenous communities are so closely linked that all the instruments relate the collective rights of indigenous peoples to environmental protection. For example, several of the international instruments on the environment and climate change address the contribution of ancestral communities, their knowledge and self-determination as part of territorial protection. The nexus between the spiritual world of several millenary and centennial communities and the material world is a transcendental aspect for these populations. For Ecuador, not only ILO Convention 169 provides for collective ethnic rights. Since 1998, the right of these communities to their ancestral territory has been recognized at the constitutional level. According to ILO Convention 169, the notion of ancestry refers to a factual connection between a specific human group whose predecessors inhabited a certain territory before the colonization of America and remain or have managed to return to that same territory today (protecting continuous or discontinuous permanence). Regarding tribal peoples, ILO (2013) explains that these are defined as:

> Their social, cultural and economic conditions distinguish them from other sectors of the national community.
> [and,]
> They are governed wholly or partly by their own customs or traditions or by special legislation.

For ILO, the precarious forms of work to which indigenous populations were subjected was an abysmally pernicious issue, so the first approach to the rights of indigenous peoples was to protect their economic rights. The forms of production and the lack of access to land due to processes of discrimination and acculturation, followed for centuries, caused the material and spiritual dispossession of these populations in large extensions of the Americas. ILO also reports that in the 1950s, there were no consistent relations between indigenous populations and workers' organizations and unions, exacerbating the precariousness of labor in the rural lands[89]. For this reason, the recognition of the relationship between these peoples and the land was the touchstone for the preservation of their culture and collective subsistence. It should be remembered that the first effort of this organization to regulate the economic situation of indigenous peoples was aimed at cultural assimilation, which largely failed because it ignored a series of social factors, among them, the cultural synergies that to this day represent a powerful challenge in interrelation and multiethnic dialogue.

The territory is more than a geographic location: it serves as a habitation and sacred place for numerous ancestral communities, which explains why its cultural, religious, social and legal importance is outstanding. Their territory serves the purpose of allowing the communities occupying it to transmit, from generation to generation, their unique customs, differentiating them from the rest of the communities and the population in general, in accordance with their worldview. Physical space in many cultures is related to the reproduction and preservation of history and the original cultural heritage, which is subject of international protection. This does not mean that without territory there is no culture, because culture is much more than a geographical location; but its high importance for the preservation of the ethnic characteristics of certain groups is a reality. Because of this, the collection of data on ancestral lands, their boundaries, the natural resources found in those, the proximity of the mestizo population (in the American case) and the relationship of all these elements with the preservation of their culture is decisive in safeguarding the collective rights of indigenous populations. Therefore, having sufficient and timely knowledge becomes an unavoidable duty for the state, which must guarantee the survival of

[89] International Labor Organization Office (2013)

ethnicities and groups that have been historically marginalized. Accordingly, only on the basis of quality information on these aspects will the state be able to generate effective public policies that respect and promote diversity and that do not result in the intensification of inequality and its consequences.

In 2011, the Ecuadorian Ombudsman's Office[90] initiated an investigation into a case involving a Shuar indigenous community living in the Limón Indanza canton (province of Morona Santiago, in the jungle region of Ecuador). The community demanded the Ministry of Environment to demarcate their Shuar ancestral territory in order to stop the continuous hostilities with the mestizo population. In addition, in the midst of ongoing confrontations between mestizo estate owners and indigenous settlements in the area, the Shuar group alleged that mestizo immigrants had illegally appropriated farms and agricultural lands that they considered part of their ancestral property. The claimants demanded that the state defined the boundaries of the ancestral territory they currently occupy and which they are convinced rightfully belongs to them by natural descent. Since 1970, when latifundia or land grabbing was prohibited and limitations on unproductive land tenure were legally established, several public entities have been in charge of verifying the ancestral possession of land throughout the country, but they failed to do so. Certainly, a topographic survey with such a socio-cultural component is not a simple task and even today it poses great challenges for any state, no matter how modern it may be –which Ecuador is not. Added to this challenge is the difficulty that the Shuar people were nomadic until the time of the Salesian evangelization, around 1950, so a rigid demarcation today could contravene their territorial connection precisely because of their traditional forms of production and subsistence. In addition, when the ancestral possession of certain territories is interrupted, it is to be expected that other indigenous and mestizo groups, who today also claim rights that are considered legitimate before the law, will generate occupations. This produces a clear outcome: culture –and the territorial link– cannot remain static throughout time. The meaning of certain elements in the past are not necessarily maintained today, and intra-community relations as well as those of the community with other ethnic groups have produced profound changes that cannot be ignored. To annul cultural reproduction and communication with other cultures would be as serious as annulling its very origin.

In the Limón Indanza case, however, it became evident that there was no methodology to address this issue from a rights-based and intercultural approach. After the intervention of the Ombudsman's Office, it was found

[90] Aso. Campesinos Limón Indanza v. SSTRA 2011.

that none of the institutions responsible for generating this information[91] had actually carried out the required studies to tackle the problem. The information on ancestral and collective land ownership empowers an indigenous community to demand respect for their fundamental rights, their express participation in certain public decisions, and the protection of their collective identity, culture and history. In short, to claim their place on Earth. Through this recognition, these peoples can, in turn, exercise their self-determination by making their own decisions regarding their development model characterized by the indigenous cosmovision, in which production and nourishment are often not individualistic but communal. Due to the lack of accurate and truthful information, the legal status of this indigenous nationality (and various others that are in similar conditions) remains uncertain within a legal and political system predominantly controlled by the mestizo population, which holds national authority.

The question of who holds official authority is not a minor one, as it defines how the conflict will be addressed and, often, the shape and size it will take. The intercultural and dialogue approach, for example, has advantages in defining strategies to reduce confrontation and harmonize the vision of an ethnic group with that of the majority of the population. These methodologies do not always converge with the traditional democracy of majorities on which Western states are based. However, they prove to be timely and effective in the face of lessons from ethnic conflicts in Europe and Africa in which *minorities* are mobilizing for secession[92]. In America, on the other hand, ethnic groups are not seeking independence as a nation but recognition as political and social actors. This gives rise to tensions with the majority state (which in the Americas, is, in turn, mostly mestizo) and polar visions on how to manage the *res publica*, which includes the territory and its resources. Gutierrez (2013) explains that:

> A conflict is not bureaucratically neutral since it generates responsibility and guilt; it is not an accident, on the contrary, it faces a process of gestation, maturation and outcome. The ethnic population is usually more prone to harm, due to the lack of institutional protection and complicity with other actors (...). Harm occurs because the bureaucracy acts with inefficiency, ambiguity or lack of interest. Harm is often justified because there are serious absences: lack of coordination between government agencies, lack of logistics to provide protection, lack of financial and human resources; in short, lack of institutional coherence (Gutierrez Chong 2013, 40-41).

[91] The National Heritage Institute, the former Secretariat of the Peoples and the Ministry of the Environment, according to the investigative file (Aso. Campesinos Limón Indanza v. SSTRA 2011).

[92] Gutiérrez Chong 2013.

In addition, the absence or poor representation of ethnicity in public bodies necessarily leads to confrontation because the voice of ethnic diversity has no echo in the public structure.

All the deficiencies detected by Gutierrez can be verified in the absence of complete and sufficient information that aggravates the ethnic social conflict. In the case mentioned above, the lack of technical tools to gather territorial and cultural information about the Shuar community was noticeable, but it is aggravated by the fact that the conflict is seen from the state (meaning, from the public officers) as a matter of *others*, not of *us,* because it is understood that it is not an issue that concerns the general population but a *small* part of it. However, if it had been a border problem between cantons or *mestizo* parishes, it could have had a different approach from the authorities. A reflection of this is the case of the Mapuche people who sued Chile before the IACrtHR for violations of the right to a fair trial, as several indigenous leaders were convicted as terrorists without evidence to support such a severe charge. As Bengoa (2016) relates, the discrimination of the non-indigenous population fueled the fire and helped to worsen an already complex situation regarding the disputed land possession between the Mapuche indigenous people and mestizo landowners, and for which the state had not designed a solution:

> Not few media outlets irresponsibly stoked the fire; not few courts irresponsibly condemned Mapuche leaders for unfounded causes and reasons; not few landowners were happy that Mr. Figueroa and his sister condemned their historic neighbors, with whom they surely played as children, to the pains of hell. Finally, an analysis should be made of how the authorities, many of whom had also suffered violations of their rights during the Dictatorship, had so little responsibility that they decreed that the Mapuche were terrorists for demanding the lands that had been taken from them. (Bengoa 2016, 239)

The Mapuche conflict also thrived from the lack of attention to boundary issues and a definitive solution to the overlapping property rights (claimed as ancestral by the community, on the one hand, and in legitimate possession according to mestizo laws, on the other). The conflict caused years of violence and suffering that an adequate public policy, with a multi-ethnic approach, could have resolved in a better way, avoiding violence escalate.

These are just a couple of examples of the hundreds of cases in which a point of confrontation between the state and an ethnic group has as its critical node information, or rather, the absence of it. Because of their profound relationship with the land, conflicts involving the interests of ancestral communities often –not always– have a strong environmental component. Therefore, access to quality, complete, verified and timely environmental information becomes transcendental for the protection of rights but also to reduce tensions that, due to the lack of a technical and intercultural approach, end up leading to violence and inequality, among other failures.

On the other side, however, there is the reinvention caused by the indigenous emergency, which can dilute the decades of advancement of the collective rights of ethnic communities, and which can be just as harmful as the very disregard of the collective rights of ancestral communities. And it is not that culture must remain static to be considered culture or to maintain the character of ancestral –it is impossible for it to *be* static![93]– but that the right of ancestral peoples must be applied distinguishing those forms of life that require this protected cultural preservation because not all cultures are in the same situation of vulnerability. The point of inflection is that indigenous communities do not have rights different from those of the rest of the population but, due to historical and systematic discrimination, their culture reached a point of crisis in which the Law had to form a margin of protection to prevent their disappearance. This is achieved through modalities of exercise of rights applied to the specific situation, through affirmative actions and principles that allow the prevalence of the rights of these populations before others. In short, collective rights allow for an equal treatment of universal rights of ethnic groups.

> Indigenous peoples' rights are not "special" rights, but articulate the universal human rights that apply to indigenous peoples. This means that it is important to contextualize the rights to the situation of indigenous peoples

[93] Pino (1993, 114) recounts one of the oldest indigenous customs that has permeated mestizo society and continues to this day: "*In Tucumán [Argentina] there subsist in popular memory, albeit unconsciously, adherence to the laws of the Incanato, now converted into customs. One of them is that of solidarity and community work. When a newcomer begins to build his ranch in the countryside or in an emergency village, he immediately receives the help of the other neighbors, but he is morally obliged to behave in the same way when he sees someone else building his house. Nowadays this custom is called "la ayudada" and is a reminder of the "minga" in pre-Hispanic times*. This is a simple example of the conversation between different cultures that coexist and feed each other.

In contrast, to preserve intact a culture voluntary isolation of entire communities is also guaranteed by states. However, even the uncontacted peoples have been influenced by the everchanging conditions of the *exterior*, needing to defend their territory and ways of living from different intruders throughout history. Nevertheless, the attempt of "pure preservation" of a culture may lead to its disappearance, like in the case of the "Lost Woman of San Nicolas", or as is rapidly occurring with the people of Uros in Bolivia.

> and to take into account their collective aspects. For example, indigenous children have the same right to education as all other children, but their different languages, histories, knowledge, values and aspirations must be reflected in educational programs and services. In this sense, the Convention provides for special measures to ensure effective equality between indigenous peoples and all other sectors of a given society. However, the requirement for special measures does not mean that the Convention provides for special privileges to be granted to indigenous peoples with respect to the rest of the population (International Labor Organization Office 2013, 3).

That set of specific measures to ensure material equality must fulfill its purpose. From then on, once the conditions of vulnerability are overcome, rights are equalized and then, once the bridge is built, specific actions lose their raison d'être. This intercultural dialogue is, in fact, one of the symptoms that humanity is moving towards the desired point of equilibrium, equality and non-discrimination postulated by human rights instruments, although the journey is long, and the goal still seems distant. There are no right or wrong ways for this interrelation as long as the dignity of all the stakeholders is respected in the dialogue.

> The main characteristic of the indigenous emergence is the existence of a new identity discourse, that is, a "reinvented indigenous culture". It is an "urban reading" of the indigenous tradition, carried out by the indigenous people themselves, according to their own interests and objectives. That is why it is a discourse of ethnic identity deeply rooted in tradition, but with the capacity to leave it and dialogue with modernity. We could characterize this reconstruction with the following elements. It is an identity that makes it possible to build a bridge between traditional cultures, which are "those who know", and urban indigenous cultures, which are "those who remember". It produces an indigenous culture appropriate to the new stage of modernization that Latin American countries are going through (Bengoa 2016, 96-97).

Beyond ethnic collective rights, there is a threat that produces harmful effects on both the mestizo and indigenous populations (and on the latter, in a differentiated manner due to their own characteristics and the hermeticism produced by the lack of intercultural tools). This is the denaturalization of the collective rights of ethnic communities. The rights recognized to indigenous and tribal peoples are denaturalized when those who are not entitled to them slip through the cracks to take advantage of the margin of action that comes with belonging to an ethnic group, to take unrightful advantage of the legal recognition of collective rights. And the harmful aspect is that the hard core of this group of rights is diluted in objectives that have no relation whatsoever with the protection of culture and cosmovision, but serve other political, economic and even, intentionally or unintentionally, criminal objectives. Such is the case of Ecuarunari et. al. v. Ministry of Mines (2018), in which the administration of justice of Ecuador ordered the suspension of the activities of a mine concessioned to a Chinese consortium after hearing a case on the right to prior consultation of the indigenous peoples of Molleturo. The sentence did not elucidate the ancestral character of the population of the sector or their relationship with the land on which the project was being developed, but still ordered –in the first instance[94]– the suspension of the mining project until the state undertook the prior consultation established in ILO Convention 169. Only a few days after the judicial suspension, armed groups of illegal miners took over the company's facilities and started gold extraction, sowing terror among the population and provoking grave environmental damage still to be fully assessed. So far, neither the communities surrounding the mine nor the population of Ecuador have benefited from the minerals in the subsoil, but only the unstoppable machinery of organized crime[95]. The suspension of activities, the abandonment of the facilities and the presence of illegal groups have exacerbated the socio-environmental conflict among the already divided inhabitants of Molleturo, escalating to levels of violence alien to these peaceful moorland communities. The political leaders who brought the legal actions against the Chinese mining company have not shown the same effort to demand security in the territory and the state does not present a solution to the environmental conflict or the violence, demonstrating, rather, a lack of resources. Logically, as there is no authorization to extract minerals, there is no environmental management plan or accurate studies on the level of harm being caused, nor has the illegal activity been firmly eradicated, but on the contrary, domination is maintained by those who have abused a recognized human right of the indigenous populations. This raised a new form of violation of the right to information: the lack of timely information on the situation of potential insecurity that should have been foreseen by judges and public forces, as well as the absence of real data on the damage that is being caused. These circumstances, added to the lack of sufficient dissemination about the mining project under state authorization, which initially worsened the level of rejection on the part of the communities, have led to an environmental and social disaster.

The UN Development Declaration provides that peoples have the right to benefit economically from the natural resources found in their territories.

---

[94] As of the date of publication of this book, the case is still awaiting final judgment by the Constitutional Court of Ecuador.

[95] Beltran 2022.

But as illegal activities are the only ones profiting from the subsoil resources in this and numerous similar cases, neither the community nor the country are benefitting from the value of these resources; taxes are not being collected, and instead of generating social services for the community, it is plunging into a crude spiral of violence, prostitution and marginalization. Although the state is also the guarantor of public security (including prevention) and the prosecution and punishment of illicit activities, the reality is that this also requires resources[96], training and strategy that have proven to be insufficient to mitigate the effects of the war for minerals that has already begun in these territories. The Rio de Janeiro Declaration, in Principle 5[97], also postulates the eradication of poverty and the reduction of disparities as an integral part of sustainable development policies. In this manner, the economic growth of natural resource exporting countries must be appropriately considered by states and corporations, in order to meet the environmental and social costs that accompany the extraction of non-renewable natural resources, which is only possible if the state assumes control of those resources and their productive chain, and these activities are framed within the law.

Discussing collective rights and access to information within ancestral communities requires addressing the case of Pueblo Indígena Sarayaku v. Ecuador (2012) resolved by the IACrtHR. This prominent case related to the administration of environmental justice also generated a set of minimum, essential requirements related to the dissemination of the information necessary to accurately assess the effects of a specific project on the way of life of an indigenous community and to ensure their involvement in public decision-making. Previously, in the cases of Moiwana Community (2000)

---

[96] In this regard, Holmes and Sunstein (2011, 63-65) explain that rights are not reached by spontaneous reproduction, they require financial investment to achieve their ends:

> *"Where there is a right, there is a remedy' (...) rights that are legally enforced are necessarily positive. (...) All rights are costly because they presuppose an effective oversight machinery, paid for by taxpayers, to monitor and control. (...) The financing of basic rights through revenues derived from taxes helps us to see clearly that rights are public goods: social services financed by taxpayers and administered by the state to improve collective and individual well-being."*

[97] Principle 5: All States and all people shall cooperate in the essential task of eradicating poverty as an indispensable requirement for sustainable development, in order to decrease the disparities in standards of living and better meet the needs of the majority of the people of the world.

Also, Principles 12 and 16 address the issue of the economic benefits of activities that impact on the environment in states supporting the same.

and Saramaka People (2007), both against Suriname, the IACrtHR had already established that ancestral peoples have the right to ownership of the territory they occupied before the colonization of the Americas. But in Sarayaku v. Ecuador, the Court went further into the right to free, prior and informed consultation on decisions that may affect indigenous communities in relation to the environment or their social structure, on the understanding that the sociocultural development of the indigenous community depends on the territory it occupies and that the people belong to that territory, and viceversa. Therefore, the tension between land ownership (constitutionally and legally recognized to the communities) and subsoil resources (inalienable property of the state, according to the Ecuadorian Constitution) calls for dialogue to agree on how to guarantee the right to development of these communities without leaving aside the right to development of the rest of the nation.

According to this ruling, the right to consultation implies no minor state restructuring:

> The obligation to consult the indigenous and tribal communities and peoples on any administrative or legislative measure that may affect their rights, as recognized under domestic and international law, as well as the obligation to guarantee the rights of indigenous peoples to participate in decisions on matters that concern their interests, is directly related to the general obligation to guarantee the free and full exercise of the rights recognized in the Convention (Article 1(1)). This entails the duty to organize appropriately the entire government apparatus and, in general, all the organizations through which public power is exercised, so that they are capable of legally guaranteeing the free and full exercise of those rights[98].

This obligation to accommodate the state structure to guarantee the rights of indigenous peoples is not unrelated to the production and effective dissemination of information. It goes beyond opening the debate to the inhabitants of the territory in which a specific project is to be developed, but rather requires leveling the playing field so that their opinions count. Therefore, the state's duty is not limited to providing information, but the purpose of providing information must be to guarantee the real participation of the native peoples. According to the Court, the minimum information for this purpose is that developed by the UN Permanent Forum on Indigenous Issues[99]:

---

[98] Sarayaku Indigenous People v. Ecuador 2012, para. 166.

[99] Report of the International Workshop on Methodologies regarding Free, Prior and Informed Consent and Indigenous Peoples, E/C.19/2005/3, 17 February 2005.

- The nature, size, pace, reversibility, and scope of any proposed project or activity;
- The reason(s) or object(s) of the project and/or activity;
- The duration of the foregoing;
- The locations of the areas that will be affected;
- A preliminary assessment of the likely economic, social, cultural and environmental impact, including potential risks and a fair and equitable distribution of benefits in a context that respects the precautionary principle.
- Personnel likely to be involved in the implementation of the proposed project (including indigenous peoples, private sector personnel, research institutions, government employees, and others);
- Procedures that may be involved in the project

International instruments dealing with the safety of the environment repeatedly insist on the need for states to promote citizen participation in making decisions that affect the environment, to produce sufficient and quality information to generate public debate, and to disseminate such information, as well as any other information required for this purpose.

States, therefore, share responsibility for environmental protection with the citizenry and open the decision-making processes to citizen oversight from the very genesis of the public decision. This does not mean in any way that the population can be held responsible for the effects or damage to the environment, but rather that a form of self-regulation is generated on both sides: the state and civil society. Together they can purport to much more stable ground rules for large industries, provided that all parties participate in good faith. The population is also expected to stay in permanent citizen oversight, since the process of participation does not end with the issuance of a public authorization but continues throughout the life of the project and certain period of time after its closing. Indigenous communities play an important role as social actors in this scenario, considering their long trajectory with the land.

The Relationship between Information and Access to Justice

Access to justice is the ability of individuals to seek and obtain a fair and effective resolution to their legal disputes. It encompasses not only the formal right to file a lawsuit or press charges, but also the practical ability to navigate the legal system and receive a balanced outcome, obtain redress for harm, and hold wrongdoers accountable. The administration of justice is one of the pillars of the structure and organization of the state and of democracy. Historically, the act of entrusting the resolution of a dispute to an impartial and meritorious third party was considered a civilized approach to reaching agreements, avoiding violence and promoting social peace. During the Roman Empire –whose legal structure is the ancestor of the modern continental legal system– access to justice was strictly regulated. The responsibility of defending and judging cases was entrusted to those considered the most qualified persons and was limited to Roman citizens, so that persons not considered as such were deprived of judicial recourse.

The process, understood as a set of steps that lead the parties and the judge to the culmination of a controversy through a decision by an objective and impartial third party (the judge as representative of the state, acting on behalf of the people) has the ultimate purpose of ensuring the administration of justice in an impartial manner, *to render to every man his due (dare cuique suum)*. But when the process becomes a Kafkaesque labyrinth[100] that does not obey justice because it condemns the innocent and leaves the guilty unpunished, it loses its authority as the foundation of the democratic state. The publicity of court records sheds light on what the operators of justice are doing in the name of the people and in (supposed) benefit of society. But it is far from being the only way to ensure fairness and for that the parties must be in a truly equal position to act within the winding path that justice outlines to guarantee its purpose.

Today, the right to access to justice is a legal protection that is explicitly included in several international human rights covenants, such as the Universal Declaration of Human Rights, the International Covenant on Civil and Political Rights, the African Charter on Human and Peoples' Rights, and, of course, the European and American Conventions on Human Rights. All of these explicitly recognize the right of access to justice by establishing minimum rules to ensure the protection of the innocent and due process for

---

[100] In Franz Kafka's "The Trial", the protagonist K, entangled in an unintelligible process on which his life hung, in the hands of an old lawyer who never got out of bed to defend him and who never did anything to explain the system to him, is a character replicated thousands of times, daily in the courts of justice. In the midst of the procedural maze through which K wanders uselessly, this dialogue takes place in which the publicity of the judicial proceedings becomes relevant:

> *Painter - The sentences handed down by the courts are not only not made public, but even the judges themselves do not have the right to see them, so that only legends about the justice of the past have been preserved. These legends speak of true acquittals, and not of nothing, but of many.*
>
> *K. - This fully confirms my opinion of justice. So I cannot have any hope for my innocence either. The court is unnecessary. It suffices only an executioner to replace it.* (Kafka 1996, 199).

everyone. This right has been further elaborated by domestic legislation through procedural rules for the guarantee of a *fair trial*, as the simple act of filing a lawsuit or pressing charges for civil or criminal disputes does not qualify as access to justice *per se*. Governments are obliged to provide a series of guarantees to ensure the realization of this right from, not only from a formal but also from the substantive perspective. Such guarantees include the impartiality and independence that must characterize judicial systems, the provision of free legal aid and representation to those who cannot afford it, the removal of barriers that prevent marginalized groups from accessing justice, and minimum standards that order the process toward a primary end, which is the finding of the truth for the resolution of a conflict. Article 6 of the European Convention on Human Rights assures individuals:

> Article 6
> Right to a fair trial
> In the determination of his civil rights and obligations or of any criminal charge against him, everyone is entitled to a fair and public hearing within a reasonable time by an independent and impartial tribunal established by law. Judgment shall be pronounced publicly but the press and public may be excluded from all or part of the trial in the interests of morals, public order or national security in a democratic society, where the interests of juveniles or the protection of the private life of the parties so require, or to the extent strictly necessary in the opinion of the court in special circumstances where publicity would prejudice the interests of justice.

Article 8 of the American Convention on Human Rights contains some of these basic guarantees:

> Article 8. Right to a Fair Trial
> Every person has the right to a hearing, with due guarantees and within a reasonable time, by a competent, independent, and impartial tribunal, previously established by law, in the substantiation of any accusation of a criminal nature made against him or for the determination of his rights and obligations of a civil, labor, fiscal, or any other nature. (...)

As provided in Article 8.2 (c) of the American Convention[101], and Article 6.3 (b) of the European Convention[102], one of the guarantees for

---

[101] 2. Every person accused of a criminal offense has the right to be presumed innocent so long as his guilt has not been proven according to law. During the proceedings, every person is entitled, with full equality, to the following minimum guarantees: (...) c. adequate time and means for the preparation of his defense.

[102] 3. Everyone charged with a criminal offence has the following minimum rights: (b) to have adequate time and facilities for the preparation of his defence.

access to justice is the real possibility of presenting evidence as part of one's defense. In this aspect, access to information acquires utmost importance for an adequate defense, especially when the counterparty is a government authority or agency or a private party acting on behalf of the government. The Ecuadorian Constitution holds public authorities, private persons acting on behalf of or under the authorization of the state, as well as those who provide public services or services of public interest, responsible for damages caused to the fundamental rights of the population as a consequence of the exercise of public functions or the provision of public services. Therefore, when it comes to human rights litigation, the counterparty will always be the state machinery or those acting in its name. This means that the defendant party will have certain advantages over the plaintiff, particularly in relation to the information that supports the state activities that will be the aim of the dispute. Therefore, matching the positions of the opposing parties is essential to arrive at the truth of the facts.

The importance of access to information in a timely manner as a key element of access to justice becomes apparent in the work of human rights and environmental advocates, in consumer rights cases and others where the power and force of the defendant may represent a serious barrier to the fair trial standard. For such cases, domestic law provisions have generally been developed to balance the legal situation, such as the reversal of the burden of proof or the principle of dynamic proof. Yet, this does not replace the need for access to information and documentation on goods or services of importance to society (not only of a public nature) that will allow interested parties to know the truth even before there is a case of harm, violation of rights, danger to life or other legally relevant goods. Therefore, the refusal to grant access to public information or that of public interest may result in the violation of other fundamental rights, including effective judicial protection, which may lead to a breach of due process, because the interested party may be prevented from substantiating its allegations. In the case of the ECrtHR, this co-dependence has been verified in a serious manner, where it has also been shown that the state's refusal to provide information was motivated by the desire to prevent public scrutiny and accountability. The Charter of Fundamental Rights of the European Union, in Article 41, correlates the right to good public administration with the right of everyone to have access to the file concerning him or her. In other words, the realization of the right to good administration rests on the material and legal possibility of *knowing* the information that public bodies hold against a person.

Thus, it becomes apparent that information serves the individual right of defense and the arm's length principle, but also the protection of collective interests. For example, in Magyar Helsinki Bizottság v. Hungary, the state denied information on the method of appointment of public defenders that was relevant to identify possible discrimination against a sector of the population in the prosecution of criminal charges[103]. The Court, in addition to upholding the need for a public interest test (discussed in previous chapters), found that the work of private nongovernmental organizations in scrutinizing the state requires availability of the relevant information:

> It is in the interest of democratic society to enable the press to exercise its vital role of "public watchdog" in imparting information on matters of public concern (see Bladet Tromsø and Stensaas, cited above, § 59), just as it is to enable NGOs scrutinising the State to do the same thing. Given that accurate information is a tool of their trade, it will often be necessary for persons and organisations exercising watchdog functions to gain access to information in order to perform their role of reporting on matters of public interest.
> (...)
> As to the role of the applicant NGO, it is common ground between the parties that the present case concerns a well-established public-interest organisation committed to the dissemination of information on issues of human rights and the rule of law.

The protection of fundamental rights was also analyzed in the case Youth Initiative for Human Rights v. Serbia, in which factual information on electronic surveillance measures had been requested from the Serbian Intelligence Agency, which had subjected an undetermined number of inhabitants to this type of surveillance without their knowledge. The same Court found that the social function of this non-governmental organization was thereby impeded and that the refusal constituted a violation of freedom of expression:

> The Court notes that the applicant requested the intelligence agency to provide it with some factual information concerning the use of electronic surveillance measures. The agency first refused the request, relying thereby on the statutory provision applicable to secret information. After an order by the Information Commissioner that the information at issue be nevertheless disclosed, the intelligence agency notified the applicant that it did not hold that information. As the applicant was obviously involved in the legitimate

---

[103] The right to legal aid was recognized as a cornerstone of justice by, among others, the United Nations Principles and Guidelines on Access to Legal Aid in Criminal Justice Systems and Directive 2013/48/EU on the right of access to a lawyer in criminal proceedings. (...) For that reason, external scrutiny of police appointments of legal-aid lawyers was an essential guarantee of ensuring fair-trial rights under Article 6 of the Convention (Magyar Helsinki Bizottsag v. Hungary 2016, para. 95).

> gathering of information of public interest with the intention of imparting that information to the public and thereby contributing to the public debate, there has been an interference with its right to freedom of expression.

Also in Társaság a Szabadságjogokért v. Hungary, it was concluded that the role of organizations in monitoring the actions of the state is protected by the Convention. In that case, the non-governmental organization asked the Hungarian Constitutional Court for access to a file on the revision of the rules on drug offenses in the criminal code, which was denied by the high court. It is quite striking that it is precisely the domestic court concerned with guaranteeing constitutional rights that objects to access to a document from its own repository. According to one of the *amici curiae*[104] in this case, this behavior raises concerns about the right to a fair trial:

> Publicity of judicial proceedings is a fundamental tenet of the rule of law and due process. This Court has long held that, under Article 6 of the Convention, publicity of court proceedings is essential to the protection of litigants' rights and the maintenance of public confidence in the administration of justice. Therefore, any exceptions to the right to a public hearing must be construed strictly and applied in a manner proportionate to the objective pursued.
>
> Granting third parties (or the general public) access to court records, including party pleadings and submissions, may raise legitimate issues of fair trial and the need to maintain the integrity of judicial proceedings. However, court records are public records, and as with other information in the possession of the state, the public's right of access must be properly balanced against other legitimate public and private interests. Such rules of access are commonly defined in Europe by judicial and procedural codes, general access to information laws, or a combination of both. The draft Council of Europe Convention on Access to Official Documents allows restrictions on access that are "necessary in a democratic society" for protecting "the equality of parties in court proceedings and the effective administration of justice," among other interests.

Also noteworthy is Zwartveld v. Commission (1990), which pitted a European Community member state against the European Commission, when it refused to provide information to the Netherlands. The Dutch authorities were investigating a case of black-market fishing in which Dutch authorities and European Commission inspectors were allegedly involved. To get to the truth of the matter, the Dutch authorities requested the

[104] Open Society Justice Initiative, the Financial Times Ltd and Access Info Europe 2008, paras. 23-24.

Commission's assistance in finding out the identity of the fisheries inspectors who had been involved in control activities between 1983 and 1987, and to bring them to the Commission's attention. But the Commission refused. According to that organism, to do so would interfere with the functioning and independence of the European Community and jeopardize the tasks entrusted to it. The European Court of Justice ruled that withholding this information was contrary to the rule of law, which requires to ensure that the law is enforced, for which cooperation with investigative and judicial bodies is necessary. These are some of the most relevant terms to demonstrate the intrinsic relationship between information and access to justice contained in that ruling:

> The national court's request is intended solely to obtain the communication of certain information in the Commission's possession which it requires in order to exercise the powers conferred upon it by national law and does not involve any risk that the Commission will encroach upon the powers of the national authorities. (...) the Community institutions are under a duty of sincere cooperation with the judicial authorities of the Member States, which are responsible for ensuring that Community law is applied and respected in the national legal system.

In addition, the Court included among its provisions that the inspecting officers should testify, thus including not only the written information contained in the reports, but also the information contained intellectually in the inspectors' persons.

In each of these cases –which are, certainly, emblematic of the protection of the right to seek information in the European region– although the common thread of the court's analysis is freedom of expression, there is a direct relationship with the right to a fair trial. In the Serbian and Hungarian cases mentioned above, the persons subject to investigation and prosecution by the respective countries' justice systems were placed in unclear situations on which their fate and freedom would depend. In addition, according to the theory of the "fruit of the forbidden tree", the illegality of the state's actions in promoting actions against an individual can cause their nullity, so that the manner in which evidence is obtained is not a minor issue (as seen in the Serbian case). It is concluded, then, that sufficient information is highly relevant to fundamental freedoms.

For the guarantee of due process, a procedural rule that, although it may seem elementary, has proven to require the highest level of legal protection is the publicity of judicial records and proceedings. This consists of the right of access to all information in an investigative file or any other type of file that is under processing of a public authority, whether administrative or judicial, subject to the protection of trade or other types of secrets which, by their nature, should not be disseminated indiscriminately. The parties, however, can always have access to the proceedings, whether civil, criminal, administrative or any other area, because the decision will affect their rights or obligations as citizens. Therefore, prior to being resolved by a judicial or non-judicial authority, the citizen must be able to know the full content of the investigation in order to be able to defend him or herself. This is not only relevant in the criminal sphere, where often the procedural system allows the person under investigation to be kept out of the conclusions of the investigation until the case is sufficiently substantiated to allow the filing of charges, arrest or similar orders. It is also relevant in the imposition of economic, civil or political obligations, and ultimately, timely information is key to a strategic defense in the judicial arena.

In 2019 there was a case in which a private company was sanctioned by the Comptroller General of the State of Ecuador, and was ordered to pay several millions of dollars. The company requested the file to understand how the charges were confirmed, but the Comptroller's Office replied that the information was reserved because it was qualified as such in an internal resolution of this body that includes the term "working papers" in the list of undisclosable information. Note that this resolution has minimal legal power since, according to the Ecuadorian Constitution, all information of a person involved in an administrative file is accessible to him or her, in order to guarantee the right to defense. The information was denied on two occasions by the state entity without reasoning on the alleged or possible harm that the release of the information could cause, versus the harm to the right of access and even to due process, by withholding information from the private organization under investigation. The petitioner had to resort to constitutional justice to request the complete file since it was materially impossible to challenge the Comptroller's findings without understanding the propriety and truthfulness (or lack thereof) of the same within the investigative body. In the meantime, the deadline to challenge the administrative decision was still running. This case highlighted the conflict of interest in a dispute in which the state institution becomes judge and jury since, at first, it was in charge of the audit that the private entity needed to challenge and of which it would automatically become the defending party. Handing over the requested information would have leveled the ground between the parties before the judge, forcing the institution to make a more professional defense to improve its chances of winning the case. On the other hand, withholding the information until the last moment prevented the presentation of exculpatory evidence and even seriously jeopardized the filing of a lawsuit at all, leaving the administrative actions of the

Comptroller's Office unexamined. It should be noted that the universal principle of procedural good faith requires the parties to present their information in time for the opposing party to be able to contradict them, if appropriate.

Preventing people from having access to public reports hinders the public scrutiny that is natural to a democratic form of state, as has been explained. But there is an even more relevant issue and that is when public opinion, already formed, moves towards a concise position of confrontation, bringing to trial those it considers having caused damage to protected legal goods. Then, information provides for the achievement of the right to a fair trial.

Justice in the Information Society

So far, we have provided an overview of information as a means of exercising the right to a fair trial. But the right to information faces other highly important challenges. Hans Klein (2006) posits an information society that involves a whole alternate jurisdiction that overlaps with the physical one. It is not a fantasy immersed in a factual reality, but two parallel worlds with their own regimes. For this author, this society has its own political institutions, a *citizenship* that is exercised independently of geographical location or positivized legal requirements, its own economic and even tax regime, and authorities that have little to do with democracy, citing the Free and Open Source Software Movement and the Internet Corporation for Assigned Names and Numbers[105] as examples of this *de facto* power. In this context, citizen participation has developed *naturally*, without attending to express legal recognition and even prior to it. Because citizenship exists in virtuality, and because there is a digital personality in all internet participants.

> The claim that there exists an information society in its own right is most strongly made with respect to cyberspace. A not insubstantial literature makes the claim that when we log on to the Internet, we leave physical space behind and enter a different dimension of existence with unique properties and unique social relationships. (Klein 2006, 190).

Much can be developed about the information society. Its vertiginous movement to create an alternate reality prevents studies from describing it in all its complexity for now. But for the subject of this research, the issue of illegitimate intrusion into private life, prior censorship and self-

[105] Klein 2006.

incrimination as risks related to access to justice have regained space in the information exchange in this sphere.

Marzouki (2006) relates how states have been working to address and even *take advantage of* the gray lines of jurisdiction (or lack thereof) in the exchange of sidereal information. On the one hand, a sort of *information police* is being generated that censors content and decides what and how it is disseminated without being accountable to anyone, often through logarithms that, undeniably, do not obey the common good or the public interest. A monitoring role is assigned to –private– internet providers who prevent the censored subject from accessing an impartial and public court, subject to accountability and obliged to provide the highest possible protection of fundamental rights. On the other hand, *real-life* police are given ever greater *investigative* capacity to intercept communications and data, and to share it with unnatural judges of certain individuals:

> (...) the police and other law enforcement authorities have progressively seen their investigative powers growing, particularly in terms of interception of communications, search and seizure of data, and international cooperation by exchange of data, without the need for any court order. (...) these increased powers are breaching the rule of law by the violation of the 'guarantee rights.' However, they are being legitimized by a political discourse... such as the fight against terrorism to protect the security of persons and goods, the protection of human integrity and dignity, and the protection of intellectual property. It is also based on technical and practical considerations, such as the technical difficulties of enforcing the law on the Internet (Marzouki 2006, 203-204).

The issue should not be considered a problem *of others*, since everyone with access to the internet has his or her life exposed to these regulations or, more likely, to the absence of proper, democratic and public ones. What is more serious is that the liquid society makes the authorities prone to opt for the most harmful alternatives to fundamental rights and do not guarantee access to *all* public information or, in contrast, grant access to personal or intimate information. In Brazil, access to the content of e-mails was authorized to employers by a labor court, if they are sent or received through the company's domain[106]. Vianna (2010) compiles information on some of the electronic communications surveillance systems that allow information to be fed via satellite to several countries at once on the basis of international cooperation. Among them, the Echelon system aimed at "*private and economic, non-military communications*"[107] and the Carnivore system. In

---

[106] Vianna 2010.

[107] European Parliament 2001.

the face of Echelon, the countries surrendered to accept the existence of global surveillance systems and, unable to ban them, urged states to respect human rights and avoid their abuse:

> The Member States were asked to adapt their legislation on the intelligence services to the European Convention on Human Rights, by providing appropriate guarantees not only for their own citizens but also for those from third countries on the basis of a common code of conduct, and to negotiate a similar code of conduct with the USA. They were also asked to pool their communications interception resources with a view to enhancing the effectiveness of the CFSP in the areas of intelligence-gathering and the fight against terrorism, nuclear proliferation or international drug trafficking, in accordance with the provisions governing the protection of citizens' privacy and the confidentiality of business communications, and subject to monitoring by the European Parliament, the Council and the Commission. Member States were asked collectively not to abuse the intelligence services for economic ends but, in view of their involvement in the Echelon system, the United Kingdom and Germany were asked to make the authorization of further communications interception operations by US intelligence services on their territory conditional on their compliance with the ECHR (Piodi and Mombelli 2014, 41).

Marzouki (2006) mentions several provisions of the Council of Europe Cybercrime Convention to demonstrate the susceptibility of information appropriation in the electronic context, as well as the impact of the United States Patriot Act in countries around the world. In this regard, the possibility of sharing information with authorities in other countries presents both virtues and risks of enormous importance. Among the virtues, the ability to consolidate sufficient evidence on crimes against states and public morals, such as tax evasion and corruption, are major issues that usually involve several jurisdictions. In practice, these crimes are not easy to prosecute by one state at a time and, in developing countries, investigative limitations can be a precursor to impunity. For example, the Convention on Mutual Administrative Assistance in Tax Matters allows for the automatic and spontaneous exchange of information on taxes and patrimony, without the need for a prior request or court order or process, to verify the erosion of the tax base to the detriment of one of the member states[108]. This authorization seems opposed to the basic protections of civil and political rights.

---

[108] This multilateral Convention is available even to states that are not members of the Organisation for Economic Co-operation and Development (OECD), and is currently applicable to 147 jurisdictions. (OECD 2023)

But on the other hand, basic principles of due process such as that of the natural judge or that of access to evidence produce a risk and bewilderment not only in those who are being justly or unjustly prosecuted, but in society as a whole. That is the issue with human rights: when one is harmed, it affects everyone.

There is still much work to be done on digital life from a human rights perspective, even more so with respect to the information *made* public through the internet. Challenges intrinsic to its ethereal nature are rapidly arising.

ENFORCEMENT

None of what has been developed in the previous chapters would have any practical meaning if there were no resources to turn written law into an experiential reality. As has been shown throughout this research, access to public information occurs in the midst of serious tensions because the object on which the right and its correlative obligations fall is of considerable importance for the exercise of power. By accessing information on how and for what purpose the resources of the state and its powers are being used, a step is being taken towards the evaluation of public administrators that may lead to changes in the *status quo*. Therefore, it would be unrealistic to think that its exercise will be free of obstacles, although that should be the common goal of the people and the rulers. Not only because of reluctance, but also because of ignorance or a defective provision of administrative resources, access to information could be limited or even nullified. To this end, legislators are obliged to make appropriate remedies available to the people, to be activated in the face of an illegitimate or disproportionate denial of access.

The establishment of this type of legal remedy derives from the state's obligation to guarantee fundamental rights which, as explained more fully in the introductory chapter, includes acting in case of refusal. In other words, the state has the obligation to guarantee the right of access to information even when it is the state itself –in the person of an authority, institution or public official in general– that violates it. The state must be the overseer of its own actions. So much so that the Escazú Agreement provides, as part of the guarantees for environmental information, that the state must disseminate the procedure for administrative or judicial remedies that allow a third party to define whether or not a certain piece of information should be released to the public (Article 7.9).

In order to materially guarantee any human right, each state must develop legislation that sets out the path to be followed for its realization. In addition, means must be provided for public officials and authorities to be sufficiently and continuously trained. But since this is not enough, the state structure must provide judicial remedies to cease and redress any violation. In sum, the law rests on a tripod composed of (i) the norm, (ii) the obedience of public authorities, and (iii) the judicial remedy that must be activated in case of non-compliance. This allows for an adequate legal structure that can be activated individually or collectively in the face of any violation of rights or even (under certain precepts) in the face of a threat against them.

But the practical importance of the right of access to public information also requires a state supervisory authority to reduce cases of illegitimate restriction of access in a preventive as well as reactive manner. This oversight requires a highly ethical body, operating on the basis of the guiding principles of fundamental rights, with its own budget and political independence. Most countries have, in effect, a national human rights body or ombudsman to do this work. The powers provided to it are very diverse, starting with those legislations that give it a purely ethical function to those in which it is configured as a true advocate of the people and assign even a sanctioning capacity.

Information Ombudsman

States often institute public bodies dedicated to the specific oversight of the right of access to information; a sort of Ombudsman specialized in openness and access to public data. This is the option recommended by experts. The importance of an independent supervisory and regulatory body with political independence, financial and administrative autonomy is included in the Inter-American Law Model as a guarantee of the achievement of its purposes. This aspect is also addressed by jurist Villanueva (2003), who argues that such a body is indispensable in emerging democracies, in view of the fact that institutionalism is more or less weakened and the culture of administrative secrecy is ingrained. The independent regulatory entity, in the opinion of this professor, guarantees impartiality, accessibility, greater possibilities to promote the law and to improve its application each time. The Mexican case is revealing for the rest of Latin America and probably for the world. By federal law, the Federal Institute of Access to Public Information was created, which has among its competencies the capacity to:

- resolve appeals when information has been expressly or tacitly denied,
- promote the right of access (including the development of manuals on how to use the law),
- guarantee the protection of personal data,
- monitor the enforcement of regulations,
- issue recommendations to the obligated public bodies,
- issue regulations for the filing and disclosure of public information, among others.

From the above it can be seen that the Mexican model is the ideal that the Inter-American Law Model embodies in the text developed by the experts of the Americas (Mendel 2008), at least in its formal structuring.

Whether it is a body specialized in the right to information or a generic institution for the protection and promotion of human rights, certain standards must be guaranteed by the state to ensure that it will be able to act in its role as overseer of other state institutions. The competencies attributed to this entity should cover federal or sectional governments. Moreover, its objective will be to provide effective solutions to the population with the objective of putting transparency into practice. Political and financial independence, as well as the provision of sufficient personnel and materials, becomes a transcendental issue for the protection and promotion of the right. According to the Principles relating to the Status of National Institutions (Paris Principles)[109] on national human rights institutions (or Ombudsman), independence depends on ensuring sufficient resources:

> The national institution shall have an infrastructure which is suited to the smooth conduct of its activities, in particular adequate funding. The purpose of this funding should be to enable it to have its own staff and premises, in order to be independent of the Government and not be subject to financial control which might affect its independence (UN Commission on Human Rights 1993).

Following these Principles, the promotion of rights implies that national legislation, regulations and practices be harmonized with the international human rights instruments to which the state is a party, and that their application be effective. Thus, promotion has a preventive and general character, while protection is of a particular and defensive nature, when there is harm or threat of harm to a fundamental right of a particular person or group. In addition, section D of the Principles provides for a quasi-jurisdictional capacity of human rights institutions, that is, when they have the capacity to hear and prosecute complaints. Applying these principles should help the right to information body to promote and protect access in real life.

The role of the Ombudsman is not only reactive, but also allows for the prevention of harm to individual and collective rights by drawing attention to facts that deserve to be corrected. In 1996, the European Ombudsman's office conducted an investigation in which it concluded that the absence of rules governing access to public information in the countries of the Union

[109] UN Commission of Human Rights 1993.

constituted an instance of maladministration[110]. The right to good administration is recognized in the Charter of Fundamental Rights of the European Union[111]. In this sense, the work of correlating transparency with the exercise of the rights enshrined in the fundamental rights instruments – not only the Charter, but also the Community treaties and directives– was key to develop people's prerogatives.

The United Kingdom has an institution that oversees, at the same time, the right of access to public information and the protection of personal data: the Information Commissioner's Office ("ICO"). ICO is in charge of the two main issues that elevate information management to the highest legal rank: the preservation of personal information and the dissemination and access of information that is public. Regarding proactive disclosure (the publication of information without the need for a request, usually through official electronic portals), ICO approves the publication schemes in order to endorse their usefulness to the community. Secondly, it is in charge of processing complaints of denial of access by public bodies, proposed by citizens. Through this procedure, ICO can define whether the refusal is appropriate or, on the contrary, if the denial should be revoked and information should be released. This is an administrative procedure that can be appealed before the administration of justice.

In the case of Mexico and Argentina, the national institutions for the protection of rights related to information (AAIP in Argentina and INAI in Mexico) are responsible, as in UK's case, for overseeing, once again, access to public information and the protection of personal data. According to Del Solar (2008), the IFAI, for example, has a mechanism for submitting requests for access to information online, which reduces the costs associated with the processing of this type of administrative procedures, to benefit the institution and the petitioner. The author also reports the existence of a specialized agency in Ireland, Canada, Scotland, New Zealand and India, and presents the United States as a notable case (a country in which certain public information is highly shielded):

> The United States -one of the pioneering countries to have a law on the matter- approved in 2007 the biggest reform of this system, where a specialized agency was also created, called the Office of Government Information Services[112].

---

[110] Rams Ramos 2008.

[111] European Parliament 2000, Article 41.

[112] Del Solar 2008, 91

As for Ecuador, the Ombudsman was appointed to protect and promote the right of access through the Law of Transparency. In this country, there is no agency specialized in public information, which means that a single entity is in charge of the protection and promotion of all fundamental rights, with the workload that this implies. In addition, it has been given the competence to propose lawsuits for access to public information on behalf of a person, group or organization that has been unlawfully deprived of access. However, the protection of personal data is in charge of a Superintendence specifically created by the Personal Data Protection Law, which only in April 2024 appointed its first incumbent authority.

In order to understand the role of national entities for the protection of the right of access to public information, it is useful to have some basic knowledge on their level of coverage and source of funding:

	Name of Protection Entity	**Public Funding**	**Specialized Information Entity**	**Staff**	**Country's Population**
Argentina	Access to Public Information Agency[113] ("AAIP")	Yes (USD. 1,129,910 approx.)	Yes	66 employees by 2024	46.06 million approx.
Ecuador	People's Defendant of Ecuador[114] ("DPE")	Yes (USD. 3,978,074 approx.)	No	390 employees by 2024	18.38 million by 2024
Mexico	National Institute for Transparency, Access to Information and Protection of Personal Data[115] ("INAI")	Yes (USD. 12,154,872 by 2022)	Yes	(Not available)	129.39 million approx.
United Kingdom	Information Commissioner's Office[116] ("ICO")	Yes £66,000,000 through the data protection fee. £10,298,000 total grant-in-aid.	Yes	770 approx. employees by the year 2020.	67.08 million approx. by 2020

113 AAIP 2024.

114 Ombudsman's Office of Ecuador 2024.

115 INAI 2022.

116 Information Commissioner's Office 2023. The Author was unable to find information (ironically) on ICO's staff updated to the year 2024.

As can be seen, in all four cases the protection and promotion institutions have public funding, which is consistent with the state's mission to guarantee fundamental rights. In the UK, this funding comes directly from a fee collected from private entities that manage personal data, which allows for a more transparent and direct assignation of funds. However, this may mean that the allocation of financial resources could translate into a form of pressure from the dominant political class at a given moment. Moreover, the allocation of resources for the protection of rights is often seen as a *luxury* in the state budget, particularly in developing countries.

For Del Solar (2008), the institutionalization of transparency requires a pro-transparency institutional reform, otherwise its sustainability will not be achieved. Even the appointment of an ombudsman for access and resource allocation is not enough for this author.

> As there is a "concentration of diffuse costs and benefits" in the exercise of transparency, there should be a growing demand for information that overcomes the incentives Stiglitz (2002) refers to in favor of secrecy (...) Finally, the creation of this type of bodies is consistent with the existence of ad hoc institutions to fight corruption in countries that have addressed the problem institutionally, such as Singapore, Hong Kong and Botwsana (Del Solar, 2008, 131-136).

Therefore, it is not enough to create institutions *on paper*; in order to give them life, a political and administrative change is required, of which civil society will be the main driving force.

Judicial Mechanisms

For all fundamental rights it is imperative to have a judicial mechanism to enforce the rules written in treaties and laws. A relevant point of Ecuadorian law is that it has established, at the constitutional level, an autonomous judicial remedy for access to information[117], within the catalog of jurisdictional guarantees. This is a remedy of the highest level that takes precedence, in terms of time and form of processing, over ordinary judicial venues. In addition, the Ombudsman was given the legal capacity to activate, on behalf of any citizen or the Nature, any of the judicial guarantees of constitutional rank, including that of access to public information. This, under the understanding that a matter that concerns this human right must be processed with the priority that the issue deserves. This does not necessarily pair with an efficient delivery of the information, but evidently the less time spent in

[117] Ecuador. Constituent Assembly 2008, Article 91.

administrative and judicial processes to achieve the goal will result in the greater usefulness of the information. In the case of DPE v. Comité Interinstitucional (2023), Patricia Ochoa, widow of General Jorge Gabela, denounced an alleged state crime in connection with the death of her husband, who was commander of the Ecuadorian Air Force and had accused alleged acts of corruption at the highest level. In 2012, an Inter-Institutional Committee was formed especially to investigate the case, but the final report was not made public, not even to the family of General Gabela. The Ombudsman proposed an action for access to public information against the Inter-Institutional Committee in April 2018. In the framework of this legal action, the Presidency of the Republic delivered part of the information, but not all of it, with which the ordinary justice was satisfied in first and second instances, as ruled in August 2018. Here we observe a first achievement: obtaining part of the required information on such a highly sensitive issue for the state and the population in the span of four months, when it had not been transparent for years. Nonetheless, the Ombudsman agreed to a last procedural recourse before the Constitutional Court, which, in 2023, declared that the right of access to public information was violated and ordered the release of the complete file because it is an element of the *right to truth*, which has both an individual and a collective dimension. The Court also expressed that the delivery of incomplete or inconsistent information violates the right of access, which, in case of human rights violations –as the death of General Gabela is presumed to be– can never be denied. Finally, the Court also refered that, the fact that the criminal investigation of this decease was supported with public resources, rendered the information as property of the people.

Meanwhile, in Argentina, decisions on access to public information in the courts must be processed before the federal administrative court, which handles all disputes that citizens have before any public administration, or through an action for protection of constitutional rights. As reflected in the case Giustiniani v. Y.P.F. S.A. (2015), the time factor plays an important role. In that case, Ruben Giustiniani had requested, in 2013, an investment contract between the Argentine oil company Y.P.F. and Chevron Corporation. The capital of Y.P.F. is 51% owned by the Argentine state and its general manager was appointed by the then President of Argentina, and is the same Minister of Economy, which, together with several other considerations of the Court, indicated that the information produced by the latter is public property. The information had been denied by Y.P.F. and later by the ordinary courts too, on the grounds that it could jeopardize industrial secrets, which was the original response of the oil company, and that the rights of a third party, Chevron, a private entity, would be put at risk. The Supreme Court concluded that Chevron must have known that it was dealing with a public entity and that, as a consequence thereto, its business information would also be considered public.

The cases included in this chapter are just a sample of how the right of access to public information has been embedded in the state structure. It is already a system that has (i) a (more or less) independent administrative entity capable of pointing out cases of illegitimate denial and (ii) an agile judicial recourse that can guaranty the exercise of the right by the citizenry through ordering timely delivery of complete and truthful information. Thus, it is possible to appreciate the implementation of a true institutionalization of law as a form of containment of state power and direction of the exercise of public functions.

Access to Public Information Action

Several countries have instituted a judicial mechanism that is available before the denial of a request for access by an obligated entity, in addition to the administrative mechanisms conducted by the information Ombudsman or other similar authority. The establishment of these remedies is not foreign to international law. Among the international obligations of states is that of having a suitable and effective judicial remedy –in form and time– to guarantee access. The refusal of a public body to provide information must necessarily be reviewed by a jurisdictional figure and this ruling, in turn, by a higher court. This recourse is also essential as a guarantee of the principle of review of judicial and administrative decisions, which is a basic right of due process and, therefore, must be available for all judicial rulings. In the Latin American circuit, the IACrtHR has insisted that the remedy cannot only be recognized in the law, but must also be shown to be effective:

> The Inter-American Court has established that judicial remedies are compatible with the requirements of the American Convention, provided that they are adequate and effective, that is, that they are suitable to protect the legal situation infringed, and capable of producing the result for which they were conceived. Otherwise, the lack of effectiveness of the remedy will constitute a violation of the American Convention (Special Rapporteur on Freedom of Expression 2010, para. 30).

In addition to its obvious relationship with the right of access to public information, of which it is the most eloquent guarantee, this judicial recourse is closely related to the right to petition. Following the line of analysis that places public sector entities in the capacity of administrators on behalf of the population, any request from the principal must, unfailingly, be answered, even if it is to deny it. The right to petition, which is consonant with the right to an efficient public administration, implies the responsibility and sanction of the public official who allows him or herself to ignore a citizen's petition or who addresses it without adherence to the law. In such cases, some legislations provide for administrative, judicial or punitive remedies to avoid and neutralize them. However, when the petition concerns access to information –which doctrinally belongs to the individual and not to the public administration, which is a mere holder–, specific judicial remedies have been provided. In each of the cases briefly described in the following lines, the remedies available for access to public information may be activated in the event of tacit refusal (or lack of addressment or pronouncement on a request for access) or express refusal, even if it is based on the secret, reserved or confidential nature of the information. The existence of a refusal is enough to activate a channel that allows an independent reviewer to decide whether the delivery of the information is appropriate or not.

In Argentina, as well as in Ecuador, there are specific judicial guarantees to ensure access to public information, in addition to the guarantees common to all other constitutional rights. As per the Mexican transparency law, it grants the right to appeal to the judiciary against the resolutions of the National Institute of Transparency and Access to Public Information. The judicial mechanism, in each case, elevates the discussion to a higher level and allows an impartial third party, generally outside the state functions that produced the denial, since typically, requests for information are directed to the entities of the executive branch, local governments and state-owned companies. Thus, the existence of a judicial remedy is a high, effective warrant of the right of access and is in line with the obligation to guarantee it.

In Argentina, the action for access to public information is processed before the contentious-administrative court, if the information holder is a state entity or body, or before the federal civil and commercial courts, when the information holder is a private entity. Besides, the law provides for an administrative appeal to the Agency for Access to Public Information in order to address any type of infringement of the transparency law. It's worth mentioning that this remedy is enabled not only when there is denial of access or lack of pronouncement of the obliged subject, but also when the information has been deficient or insufficient.

Access to public information in Ecuador is not only a right, but also a constitutional jurisdictional guarantee. This means that it has its own expeditious judicial procedure and purports a judicial action (the "action of access"). Due to its nature, it is processed before any ordinary judiciary body, assigned automatically when the claim is filed. This guarantees that the case is processed in a shorter time –between one and three months in practice– compared to other types of judicial proceedings involving state entities, which can take an average of five years.

In the case of the United Kingdom, a complaint about obstruction of access to information may be brought before the Information Commissioner, who, on the merits of an expeditious investigation, may issue an enforcement notice, which is appealable.

The nature of the non-suspensive effect provided for in Ecuadorian law is highly relevant. In the case of judicial action, despite the availability of an appeal, the law requires the obligated entity to comply with the judgment if it ruled in favor of the citizen, i.e., to proceed with the delivery of the information, regardless of the outcome of the appeal and even of whether such an appeal was filed or not. In contrast, the UK Freedom of Information Act provides that no authority is obliged to execute the compliance notice issued by ICO if the time limit for appeal is ongoing or (where an appeal has been lodged) if the outcome of the appeal is pending.

In short, the judicial mechanism operates as an effective guarantee of access. It is not only the action of this remedy that is useful to compel the authorities to obey the rules of access. Its mere existence and effectiveness, meaning that it proves to be an *activable* remedy in a specific jurisdiction, and not a mere normative statement, works as a behavioral modifier to direct the authorities towards compliance with the duties of transparency.

Habeas Data Action

Habeas data means to make information present. Habeas data is a constitutional guarantee of a jurisdictional nature (i.e. it is brought before the courts) available in some legislations to access, rectify, update, contextualize, eliminate[118] and ultimately, with greater or lesser restrictions,

---

[118] Although for this study the most relevant action is *access*, it is worth mentioning a brief distinction presented by the Argentine Gonzaini on each of the actions encompassed by habeas data: "*Each claim requires a different basis, because the denial of access implies not knowing the personal data that may have been stored in the defendant file; while the inaccuracy requires proof of error; the informative falsehood must indicate what it consists of and how it is to be demonstrated; the data whose suppression is requested demands verification of its origin (taking into account that 'suppression does not proceed when it could cause harm to the legitimate rights and interests of third parties, or when there is a legal obligation to keep the data).* (Gozaíni 2006, 156)"

process personal information. Although this study does not deal with the protection of personal data or its processing, this topic is very valuable for the access to certain information regardless of its reserved nature, provided that there is a link that grants ownership to the petitioner over the desired information. As noted in the previous chapter, the relationship between information and the defense at trial is transcendental for an optimal legal strategy. But this information is not available in all cases, either because it is reserved, confidential or secret, or because it does not exist. In the latter case, the action for access to public information or constitutional protection –according to the relevant legislation– can be activated to make the obliged state entity to *produce* certain information. This is the case of criminal investigations: when the investigation is insufficient or negligent, the right of access to public information may be a suitable way to compel the prosecution and the investigative police to do their job, on the basis of the precedents derived from the international courts in this regard. But in the case of confidential, secret or reserved information, this guarantee will not work. Then there remains a remedy: habeas data.

Access to personal information may be of great importance to support criminal investigations or to defend human rights. Also, in any litigation against the state or corporations acting through state delegation, there will be a need for information and documents that relate to the private person involved. Often, this information is denied because it is confidential or reserved (some cases have been cited throughout this study). However, no opposition is possible when the requested information contains personal data of the applicant. To demonstrate this legal linkage, it is necessary to prove that the data included in a certain document or file is totally or partially about the petitioner, i.e., about his/her assets, identity, family, work or professional career, etc. When this occurs, access must be open because preventing it may constitute an arbitrary interference in the private life of the person.

While for the action of access to public information no justification is required from the petitioner, because its knowledge is of public interest and derives from the democratic principle, in the case of habeas data, there is a clear demonstration requirement: the direct legal connection between the information to which access is sought and the petitioner. Additionally, habeas data is confronted with other types of state obligations, such as the protection of personal data, the safe custody of sensitive personal information and the effectiveness of certain actions such as criminal investigation or state audit. In certain jurisdictions it is required, as a general rule, that the petitioner has previously required access (or rectification, updating or cancellation, as the case may be) through administrative or non-contentious venues, and that this has been denied (this is the case of the Argentine and Ecuadorian regulations, to cite a couple of examples). Then, refusal or insufficient access will enable the recourse before the courts. It should be emphasized that in those countries where there is a body controlling the processing of personal data, access to information of this nature can be achieved by activating a complaint through those channels.

Habeas data also operates against private persons, even if they do not perform some kind of public function. For example, in a conflict between the partners of a company and their representatives, habeas data can be activated in order for a judge to order access to information that is rightfully theirs to know, if the administrators have refused to provide it. This access can allow them to call the administrators to account for the handling of information, documents, financial management, accounts and other activities that are considered private information. It can even enable the recovery of pecuniary or moral damages. The same happens with other types of information that, due to their social or economic relevance, may affect the course of an individual's life. Thus, credit records, financial data, intellectual property and other information concerning the activities of individuals must be reliable and updated in order not to cause damages or to enable the exercise of other individual rights. Hence, whoever stores this type of information, be it a public or private entity (increasingly in control of this type of data), is subject to a strict security and protection regime. On the basis of what Gozaini explains, whoever is involved in the collection of personal data willfully assumes a risky task and, therefore, is obliged by law to maintain standards of protection of that information:

> Thus, the task of storing data is not dangerous in itself, but it is dangerous when data belonging to others is stored in those files, whether or not the storage and collection process is consented to, and thus information that affects the private life and other sensitive values of individuals is disseminated to third parties. For Altmark and Molina Quiroga this compilation task is not dangerous by its nature, but it becomes so by the way it is carried out, when computer technology is used. The natural propensity to produce damage, typical of the activity in question, is such that it leads them to affirm in their qualification in terms of dangerousness (Gozaíni 2006, 158).

By virtue of this, habeas data can achieve an effective exercise of economic and social rights (even if they are not of a human-fundamental nature) and are related to the free development of personality. Situations such as those briefly described above demonstrate the importance of information for the protection of rights and interests at all levels, and for law enforcement.

In short, although habeas data cannot be activated to access public information (since there are specific mechanisms for that purpose) it is a tool for accessing data banks held by public and private entities that hold personal information of a specific individual or corporation. To activate this system can be quite useful in the field of judicial and strategic litigation.

An Unfinished Business

"*All property is impossible*", says Luigi Stornaiolo[119], and despite the reiterative discourse in this study on the need for each person to assume his or her dominion over the information that he or she is entitled to, I adhere to this truth. This phrase explains the intangibility of the right. It is an entelechy because *appropriation* does not exist naturally. There is, if anything, territorialism understood in the sense of the survival of a species that must defend –to death, if necessary– its space of subsistence and protection. Perhaps it is this space that we call "private property", without entering into the distortions of ambition, pettiness and greed, which are not commonly seen in nature either. Information, as an appropriable object, is no different from that territorial space of survival, although it is undoubtedly less palpable than the former. But its decisive influence on the living standard, on the exercise of a dignified life, makes it no different in functionality from a tree, a river or a cave where to shelter from the uncontrollable elements.

Information is an effective means of exercising other fundamental rights and freedoms. The concealment of the facts that occur every day in the public sphere fosters a climate of arbitrariness, if not systematic or serious crimes against human rights. This is demonstrated by history, which shows the omnipotent capacity of power (whether governmental, economic or of any other nature) to affect human dignity. Thus, secrecy has contributed to impunity, so it is not unreasonable to assert that its antithesis, transparency, contributes to an atmosphere of greater justice by shedding light on the activities of public administrators, even on their private activities. The authorities that govern democratic states are the true subjects of the people and of the law and are, therefore, in a position to be held accountable to their principal: the people. That is why, in the wake of the terrible cases of torture and repression in many countries, several constitutions and domestic laws have included explicit guidelines requiring the dissemination of information at all levels. Evidence of this can be found in Argentina, Mexico, Hong Kong, Singapore. The latter are proposed as examples of a generational change from a culture of high levels of corruption and poverty to one of

[119] Ecuadorian painter, in an exhibition of his works in Quito, about ten years ago.

transparency, demonstrating its importance for democracy and for economic and social stability.

Although these laws may now be taken for granted, they were the result of the struggle for recognition of human rights and resistance to the secrecy that fosters corruption and authoritarianism. In situations such as these, it is obvious that the prompt provision of information is essential for the protection of other rights and for the broader development of the personality. In a climate of legal certainty and government transparency, opportunities to find and carry out one's individual life project are reproduced. Moreover, in the context of social protests and for the work of human rights defenders, access to information could be imperative to defend the life and liberty of individuals. Such is the importance of correct and timely reporting of facts that, even in sensitive cases such as criminal investigations, public officials are obliged to disclose the place of detention of defendants, the maintenance of official detention rooms for interrogations, access to the prosecution file and other related documents in favor of lawyers, as well as other persons who have a direct relationship with the information surrounding the facts.

On the other hand, in less violent but equally important contexts, information allows political, economic and social decisions to be made with greater predictability of consequences. The provision of information on public projects of significant scope, with the potential to transform the way of life of a community, is of the utmost relevance so that those involved can express themselves and participate in a public decision that can change their lives and those of future generations. The close relationship between the right of access to public information and the exercise of civil and political rights, but also of economic and environmental rights, highlights their co-dependence.

Information is also linked to accountability. In order to measure the quality of the work of public administrators, there must be measurable information in terms of quality and quantity. It is necessary to insist that every authority and public official acts on behalf of third parties, the people, who can and must call them to account for their actions. Accountability is an obligation of public bodies but also a civic duty of individuals. Furthermore, public officers have been entrusted with the management of resources that belong to the people, on which all fundamental rights depend, that is, the material possibility of developing a dignified life and an individual life project. It is then, evidently, no small thing that they have to account for. The transparency laws of democratic countries, particularly those studied here, even bind private entities under certain conditions. Corporations entrusted by the state with the administration of a public resources –such as prison administration, natural resources exploitation, road management, to name a few among numerous other examples– are subject to a system of accountability and transparency similar to that to which purely public entities are subject. This does not mean that all their information automatically becomes public, but only that which is related to their delegation. Private entities and individuals that carry out activities with a high social impact are also subject to high levels of transparency and accountability. This is the case of improper public services, like financial institutions, the media, telecommunications, etc., and of those that distribute goods or services of high social importance, such as manufacturers of medicines or food products. These must certify their correct production and distribution because human lives depend on it. Something similar occurs with the licensing processes for the production of hydrocarbons and natural gas, mineral refining and agriculture. All of these, without ruling out others, are processes whose high environmental impact results in the need for greater state and social control. Hence the need of involvement of communities in decision-making in order to ensure, together, the sustainability of environmental services in the present and in the future for generations to come. This entails a challenge of which we cannot yet reach consequences, since technological progress certainly helps to mitigate environmental risks, but it also implies that, in the future, this generation will be judged by parameters that may not even exist today.

New technologies also confront the right to information and privacy with other rights stemming from human dignity. We currently live in two worlds: the real one, in which the rules are more or less clear, and the virtual one, in which emerging legal and social institutions are completely different. This virtual world is already being regulated in the *real* world, but there is no doubt about the prevalence of a code that is alien to traditional democratic institutions. In this virtual world, personal information is practically uncontrollable by its holders. This poses a serious challenge to fundamental rights like the protection of personal data, private and family life, as well as freedom of expression.

The way in which information relevant to society is sent, received and processed is on a par with information technologies. In turn, information feeds other rights and empowers their defense. In this sense, its conceptualization is far from being a finished matter and will continue to be under constant construction as historical events, social struggles and scientific progress continue to shape it.

BIBLIOGRAPHY

Abramovich, Victor, and Cristian Courtis. *El Acceso a la Información como Derecho.* 2000.

Ackerman, John M. "Más Allá del Acceso a la Información. Transparencia, Rendición de Cuentas y Estado de Derecho." By John M. [Coord.] Ackerman. Mexico D.F.: Siglo XXI, 2008.

Andrade v. SRI. 2-21-IA/23 (Constitutional Court of Ecuador, August 02, 2023).

Argentina. Senado y Cámara de Diputados. "Derecho de Acceso a la Información Pública." *Ley 27275.* Septiembre 14, 2016.

Aso. Campesinos Limón Indanza v. SSTRA. DNPrt-51151-2010-ASD (Defensoría del Pueblo del Ecuador, 2011).

Ávila Santamaría, Ramiro. *Los derechos sociales, del acceso a la información a la justiciabilidad.* Quito: Pontificia Universidad Católica del Ecuador, 2007.

Barragán, Daniel, and Andrea Sanhueza. "Artículo 7. Participación Pública en los Procesos de Toma de Decisiones Ambientales." In *Comentario al Acuerdo de Escazú sobre derechos ambientales en América Latina y el Caribe*, by Henry Jiménez Guanipa and et. al. [Ed.], 215-255. Bogota: Konrad-Adenauer-Stiftung e.V., 2023.

Bengoa, José. *La emergencia indígena en América Latina.* Santiago: Fondo de Cultura Económica, 2016.

Carbonell, Miguel. *Neoconstitucionalismo y Derechos fundamentales.* Quito: Cevallos, 2010.

Claude Reyes and Others vs. Chile. (Inter-American Court of Human Rights, Septiembre 19, 2006).

CONAIE v. MAATE. 51-23-IN/23 (Constitutional Court of Ecuador, November 09, 2023).

Convention for the Protection of Human Rights and Fundamental Freedoms. Rome: Council of Europe, 1950.

Del Solar, Felipe. "Transparencia, Corrupción y Acceso a Información Pública en Chile." In *Las Termitas del Estado. Ensayos sobre Corrupción, Transparencia y Desarrollo*, by Andrés, et. al. Solimano, 89-139. Santiago: Fondo de Cultura Económica, 2008.

DPE-DINAPROT-DESC – 54059– 2011– ASD. (Defensoría del Pueblo del Ecuador, 2012).

Dulitzky, Ariel. "El Principio de Igualdad y No Discriminación. Claroscuros de la Jurisprudencia Interamericana." *Anuario de Derechos Humanos 2007.* 2007. http://www.anuariocdh.uchile.cl.

Earth Org Movement. *earth.org.* October 6, 2022. https://earth.org/nature-rights/ (accessed March 31, 2024).

Ecuador. Asamblea Constituyente. "Constitución de la República del Ecuador." October 20, 2008.

Ecuador. Asamblea Nacional. "Ley Orgánica de Transparencia y Acceso a la Información Pública." 02 07, 2023.

European Parliament. "Official Journal of the European Communities." *Charter of Fundamental Rights of the European Union.* December 18, 2000.

—. *REPORT on the existence of a global system for the interception of private and commercial communications (ECHELON interception system) (2001/2098(INI)).* July 11, 2001. https://www.europarl.europa.eu/doceo/document/A-5-2001-0264_ES.html#_section2.

Fernandez González, María. "El Principio Constitucional de Publicidad." *Facultad de Derecho Universidad de Chile.* Septiembre 11, 2006. http://www.derecho.uchile.cl/jornadasdp/archivos/el_principio_constitucional_de_publicidad.pdf.

Fernández González, Miguel Ángel. "El principio constitucional de publicidad." *Revista de Derecho Público*, 2011: 147-165.

Fiss, Owen. "¿Tienen los servidores públicos derecho a la intimidad?" In *Más Allá del Acceso a la Información. Transparencia, Rendición de Cuentas y Estado de Derecho*, by John M. [Coord.] Ackerman, 311-323. México D.F.: Siglo XXI, 2008.

Gaskin v. The United Kingdom. 10454/83 (European Court of Human Rights, July 07, 1989).

Gomez Gallardo, Perla. "Introducción al Derecho de Acceso a la Información Pública." *Curso Virtual.* Mexico: CLAD, 2011.

Gómez Gallardo, Perla. *Introducción al Derecho de Acceso a la Información Pública.* 2010.

Goodwin v. The United Kingdom. 17488/90 (European Court of Human Rights, January 27, 1996).

Gozaíni, Osvaldo Alfredo. "El proceso de habeas data en la nueva ley de protección de datos personales - 2da. parte." *Revista Jurídica UCES*, 2006: 153-185.

Gutiérrez Chong, Natividad. "Introducción. Conflictos Étnicos y Etnonacionalismos." In *Territorios y Reconocimiento Constitucional,*

Vol. I., by Natividad [Coord.] Gutiérrez Chong, 25-66. México: Universidad Nacional Autónoma de México, 2013.

Holmes, Stephen. "Linajes del Estado de Derecho." In *Más Allá del Acceso a la Información. Transparencia, Rendición de Cuentas y Estado de Derecho*, by John M. [Coord.] Ackerman, 33-88. Mexico D.F.: Siglo XXI, 2008.

Information Commissioner's Office. *ICO.* December 8, 2023.

Inside Climate News. *insideclimatenews.org.* October 31, 2022. https://insideclimatenews.org/news/31102022/celebrating-victories-in-europe-and-south-america-the-rights-of-nature-movement-plots-strategy-in-a-time-of-crises/ (accessed March 31, 2024).

Inter-American Commission of Human Rights. "Advisory Opinion OC-23/17 Environment and Human Rights." 2017.

—. *Resolution No. 1/2020.* San José: CIDH, 2020.

Klein, Hans. "The Right to Political Participation." In *Human Rights in the Global Information Society*, by Rikke [Ed.] Frank Jorgensen, 185-196. Massachusetts: Massachusetts Institute of Technology, 2006.

Lavalle Cobo, Dolores. *Derecho de acceso a la información pública.* Buenos Aires: Astrea, 2009.

Lopez-Ayllon, Sergio. "El derecho a la información como derecho fundamental." In *Derecho a la información y derechos humanos*, by Jorge Carpizo and Miguel Carbonell, 157-181. Mexico: UNAM, 2003.

Magyar Helsinki Bizottsag v. Hungary. 18030/11 (European Court of Human Rights, November 08, 2016).

Marzouki, Meryem. "The "Guarantee Rights" for Realizing the Rule of Law." In *Human Rights in the Global Information Society*, by Rikke [Ed.] Frank Jorgensen, 197-218. Massachusetts: Massachusetts Institute of Technology, 2006.

Mendel, Toby. *El derecho a la Información en América Latina - Comparación Jurídica.* Quito: UNESCO, 2009.

México. Cámara de Diputados del H. Congreso de la Nación. "Ley Federal de Transparencia y Acceso a la Información Pública." May 09, 2016.

Mezones, Fernando. *Transparencia en la Gestión Pública, Ideas y Experiencias para su Viabilidad.* Guatemala: Magna Terra Editores S.A., 2006.

Monero Caro, María Dolores. "The right of access to public information from the constitutional perspective." *Métodos de Información*, 2020: 42-58.

Norman v. the United Kingdom. 41387/17 (European Court of Human Rights, July 06, 2021).

OECD. *Convention on Mutual Administrative Assistance in Tax Matters.* September 2023. https://www.oecd.org/ctp/exchange-of-tax-information/convention-on-mutual-administrative-assistance-in-tax-matters.htm.

Parliament of the United Kingdom. "Freedom of Information Act 2000." March 18, 2022.

Pigrau Solé, Antoni. *Acceso a la información, participación política y acceso a la justicia en materia de mdio ambiente: diez años del Convenio de Aarhus.* Barcelona: Atelier, 2008.

Piodi, Franco, and Iolanda Mombelli. *The ECHELON Affair.* Luxembourg: European Parliament, 2014.

Porras Velasco, Angélica. "La acción de acceso a la información pública." In *Apuntes de derecho procesal constitucional.*, by Juan [Ed.] Montaña Pinto, 191-222. Quito: Corte Constitucional para el Periodo de Transición, 2011.

Pueblo Indígena Sarayaku v. Ecuador. 245 (Inter-American Court of Human Rights, June 27, 2012).

Rams Ramos, Leonor. *El Derecho de Acceso a Archivos y Registros Administrativos.* Madrid: Reus, 2008.

Ríos Estavillo, Juan. "Libertad Informática y su Relación con el Derecho a la Información." In *Derecho a la Información y Derechos Humanos*, by Carbonell [Ed.] Carpizo, 183-225. Mexico: Porrúa, 2003.

Rojo Vivot, Alejandro. *Acceso a la Información.* Buenos Aires: Dunken, 2010.

Soberón Garreta, Daniela, and Carlos Trinidad Alvarado. "Artículo 5. Acceso a la Información Ambiental." In *Comentario al Acuerdo de Escazú sobre derechos ambientales en América Latina y el Caribe*, by Henry Jiménez Guanipa and [Ed.] et. al., 156-185. Bogota: Konrad-Adenauer-Stiftung e. V., 2023.

Solimano, Andrés. "La Corrupción: Motivaciones Individuales, Fallas del Estado y Desarrollo." In *Las Termitas del Estado. Ensayos sobre Corrupción, Transparencia y Desarrollo*, by Felipe, et. al. Del Solar, 57-84. Santiago: Fondo de Cultura Económica, 2008.

Special Rapporteur on Freedom of Expression. *The Right of Access to Information in the Inter-American Legal Framework.* OAS, 2010.

Sweden and Turco v Council. C-39/05 (Court of Justice of the European Union, July 01, 2008).

Társaság a Szabadságjogokért (TASZ) v. Hungary. 37374/05 (European Court of Human Rights, April 14, 2005).

Uçaryılmaz, Talya. "The Principle of Good Faith in Public International Law." In *Revista de Derecho Público*, by Estudios de Deusto, 43-59. https://doi.org/10.18543/ed-68(1)-2020pp43-59., 2020.

Uicich, Rodolfo. *Los Bancos de Datos y el Derecho a la Intimidad.* Buenos Aires: Ad-Hoc, 1999.

UNESCO. *Global Toolkit for Judicial Actors.* Paris: UNESCO, 2021.

—. *Interview with Pansy Tlakula, South Africa's Information Regulator.* September 27, 2022. https://www.unesco.org/es/articles/entrevista-con-pansy-tlakula-reguladora-de-informacion-de-sudafrica.

United Nations Committee of Human Rights. *General Opinion No. 34.* Geneva, 2011.

United Nations Human Rights Committee. *General Comment No. 34.* Geneva, 2011.

United Nations Human Rights Council. *Report on the promotion and protection of the right to freedeom of opinion and expression.* Report of the Special Rapporteur, Geneva: United Nations, 2009.

Upegui Mejía, Juan Carlos. *Transparencia Estatal y Datos Personales.* Bogotá: Universidad Externado de Colombia, 2020.

Vianna, Tulio. *Transparencia pública, opacidad rivada. El derech como instrumento de limitación al poder en la sociedad de control.* Buenos Aires: Ad-Hoc, 2010.

Villanueva, Ernesto. *Derecho de acceso a la información pública en Latinoamérica.* México: Universidad Nacional Autónoma de México, 2003.

—. *Derecho de acceso a la información pública en Latinoamérica.* Mexico: Universidad Nacional Autónoma de México, 2003.

Zwartveld v. Commission. C-2/88 (European Court of Justice of the European Community, December 06, 1990).